FEELING GOOD

Feeling Good

All The Time

JACK RANDALL COOK

Copyright © 2024 by Jack Randall Cook

All rights reserved. No part of this publication may be reproduced, distributed or transmitted in any form or by any means, including photocopying, recording, or other electronic or mechanical methods, without the prior written permission of the publisher, except in the case of brief quotations embodied in critical reviews and certain other noncommercial uses permitted by copyright law. For permission requests, write to the publisher, addressed "Attention: Permissions Coordinator," at the address below.

Jack Randall Cook / Author's Tranquility Press
3900 N Commerce Dr. Suite 300 #1255
Atlanta, GA 30344
www.authorstranquilitypress.com

Ordering Information:
Quantity sales. Special discounts are available on quantity purchases by corporations, associations, and others. For details, contact the "Special Sales Department" at the address above.

Feeling Good / Jack Randall Cook
Hardback: 978-1-964037-81-3
Paperback: 978-1-964037-56-1
eBook: 978-1-964037-57-8

Contents

Chapter 1   Feeling Good 1
Chapter 2   My Early Years 7
Chapter 3   The Move To The City 15
Chapter 4   My Youth, Girls, And Marriage 25
Chapter 5   Little Children . . . God's Gift 31
Chapter 6   My Little Girl Janet 33
Chapter 7   Randall J 40
Chapter 8   Jeffrey Glenn 47
Chapter 9   I'm So Grateful For God's Grace 53
Chapter 10 My Special Angel 69
Chapter 11 Our First Home, Good Times, Great Ending 78
Chapter 12 Living Fear Free 88
Chapter 13 Beginning A New Career 94
Chapter 14 Short Flight, Lasting Results 104
Chapter 15 Grandchildren And Great Grandchildren 112
Chapter 16 Retirement, Well, Kind Of 117

Chapter 1

Feeling Good

For the past twenty years, I have been sharing with people across the country about why "I feel good . . . all the time." Whether it was to a group of thirty elementary schoolteachers or more than a hundred newspaper employees, I shared my story with as much enthusiasm as possible. The list of people from different walks of life seems endless, such as a group of nurses, also I have shared it with hairdressers, and it was my privilege to speak on two occasions at the Amway corporation's headquarters on why I feel good even at work. Perhaps, though, the largest and most frequent audience to whom I have spoken have been the people who clean and maintain buildings and grounds. This is because it is the industry that I have hired, trained, and motivated salespeople to sell equipment and supplies to.

I have enjoyed sharing this topic with people of all ages, educational backgrounds, and family responsibilities, people that I am sure are facing or will be faced with difficult times. I believe that all of us, from time to time, are faced with challenges, challenges that will stretch us to and sometimes beyond what we believe our limits are. We will need to use everything available to us to overcome defeat and earn victory, to reach up, to think back, as well as to look forward, seeking every opportunity available to achieve success. Oftentimes hardship is thrust upon us without warning. Situations and/or actions of others will require us to be prepared to react. It will be our ability to react that will provide the courage necessary to give us the victory that we long for. After all, we will be remembered more for our reactions than our actions.

I believe that *feeling good* is a state of mind that requires not only discipline, but practice as well. To feel good begins on the inside. It is, I believe, necessary to feel good about oneself before we can feel good about life and about living. Although it is possible to fool others into believing that everything is fine, it is impossible to fool ourselves. To *feel good* in the context that I am referring to requires us to start from within, to seek internal peace and find contentment. In a seminar, I share with people how amazed they will be to see what they can endure when they have peace within, when we believe that life is good, regardless of the circumstances of the moment, when we understand that the "book" that gives us instructions on how to live teaches us that learning to live and to really enjoy life requires that we understand the purpose of life. When there is peace within, peace between the Creator and the created, I believe that only then can we truly *feel good*. We can feel good at work, at play, during good times, and even when life's challenges are upon us.

During the course of these seminars, I try to share my faith without preaching or insulting anyone. However, it is my belief in God and the constant striving to understand his plan for my life that motivates me to be able to *feel good*, to be able to overcome the temptation of accepting discouragement, discomfort, or defeat as the best that God has for me.

From the very beginning, I have shared with my audiences that I believe that we need to laugh more, and I invite them to during the next forty minutes to laugh—at me or with me. My goal is to just get them laughing, perhaps even at themselves. You see, we all take ourselves too seriously, we need to just lighten up a little, and although the jokes that they will hear, without a doubt, they have heard before, they still laugh. They laugh because they need to laugh, and I believe that if I give the invitation, most people will relax and just let it happen. Next, I ask for a show of hands of all those who have written or have begun to write their autobiography. I believe everyone should write their autobiography, even if they are the only one who reads it. As we think back on our life, the

Feeling Good

victories we have won, the mountains we have successfully scaled, the deep valleys that we have somehow made it through, when we consider that this road we travel is not without sharp curves, it has steep grades to climb, there are potholes to dodge, and around the bend one day we will come face-to-face with a huge boulder, it will be during those times that we will learn how prepared we are to react to difficult situations that life tests us with. It will be then that we will need to draw on the victories of the past. It is then that we will be reminded of the mountains we have already climbed, the deep dark valleys that we have made it through. But what about that large boulder that is in our roadway of life, the one that we come face-to-face with?

I would like to share with you a true story that I heard years ago. In the middle 1960s, there was tremendous population growth in the mountains of the Pacific Palisades, an area that is along the coast of Southern California, just a few miles south of Los Angeles. Through this community, which consisted of mostly beautiful mountainside homes, where some of the wealthiest people in California lived, ran California State Highway 101. Because of the population and additional tourist growth, it was decided to widen Highway 101. After several years of detours and traffic backups, the project was finally completed. After the final inspection, the newly-widened highway was opened to traffic. About 3 miles outside of one of the small villages, up on the mountainside on a flat spot, rested a huge boulder. The local residents requested that testing be done to make sure that the boulder wouldn't roll down the mountain and injure someone. The highway's department of engineers, after intensive testing, pronounced the rock unmovable and the highway safe for passage.

At the regular meeting of the local Tuesday morning bridge club, the concern about that large boulder rolling down on the highway came up for discussion again. After a great deal of chatter, one of the ladies told of her relationship with a local judge. She told her friends that she would be able to have her friend, the judge, order the highway department to have that boulder removed. And she did ask the judge, and he grated her request and gave a court order, demanding that the highway department close the highway until the boulder was removed and the potential danger eliminated.

Well, in obedience to the court order, Highway 101 was shut down, and the state sent out several engineers and highway department workers, along with a crane, flatbed truck, and a large bulldozer, to dislodge the boulder and to remove the potential danger to passing motorists. The bulldozer began to push on the boulder but was unable to dislodge it from its resting place on the flat spot above the highway. So a second bulldozer was brought to the site. The second bulldozer pushed on the first bulldozer, but even with both of them using all their power, they could not even budge the large rock. After several hours of head-scratching and idea-sharing by the engineers, it was decided to call in one of the large helicopters from the marine base located just a few miles away.
   The helicopter was attached to the boulder with cables, and with the helicopter lifting with all its power and both bulldozers pushing, the boulder finally rolled down the mountain and came to rest right in the middle of Highway 101.
   Once again, the engineers stood scratching their heads and discussing what they would do with this huge boulder sitting there in the middle of the highway. During their discussion, a young man walked up to them and asked, "What would you take for this rock?"

   With astonishment, the chief engineer replied, "You can have it, young man. Where would you like us to take it for you?"
   The young man asked them to deliver it to the parking lot of a shopping mall just down the highway, about 3 miles away, on the edge of the small village. While they were loading the rock onto the flatbed truck, preparing to bring it to the parking lot, the young man went to the mall ahead of them. He went to each store explaining that he was a sculpture artist, and for a small contribution, he would attract customers to their store by turning the huge rock into the likeness of a famous person. The merchants all liked the idea and promised him money in return for his art project.
   The young artist began his work. Just as he promised, more and more curious people came to look at his work that was good for business. After several days, as the boulder began to take shape, one of the store owners suggested that they surround the artist and his work with a

tarp to hide his work. This, he said, would cause people to be more curious as to whom the rock was going to look like, so they constructed a covered fence around the boulder and the artist. Finally, the work was completed, and the unveiling was scheduled. A large crowd gathered in the mall parking lot, including television and newspaper reporters. When the tarp was removed, there was a beautiful, rugged, bigger-than-life statue of John Wayne.

The picture of the statue was in all the newspapers in Southern California and also on the evening news. At that time, John Wayne was in a local hospital fighting for his life, suffering from lung cancer. He saw the news, read the papers, and told his family that he wanted to see the statue.

He was taken to the shopping mall by ambulance, where he announced that he liked the young artist's work. The Associated Press sent throughout the country the story of his traveling to see the likeness of himself. In Texas, a man by the name of J. Paul Getty read the article. He not only was a big fan of John Wayne but one of the richest people in the world. He sent one of his aides to purchase the statue.

When the agent of Mr. Getty, the multimillionaire oil tycoon, met the artist, he gave him half-million dollars for the statue. He called Mr. Getty and asked him where he wanted the statue. Mr. Getty said that he wanted it placed outdoors somewhere that would allow John Wayne's fans to be able to enjoy it. So the people in the small village formed a search committee. After several weeks, it was decided to place the statue about 3 miles outside the village, up on the mountainside above Highway 101, where there was a flat spot. Everyone, even the members of the Tuesday morning bridge club, thought it was the perfect place for the statue.

I have shared this long but true story to emphasize that each of us will, in our lifetime, find a large boulder blocking our way as we travel the roadway of life. Because we have practiced our reaction, as we dodged the potholes, climbed the mountains, traveled through the deep valleys, and because we have already overcome various difficulties, we will look at the boulder that is in our roadway either as an obstacle, as the highway workers did, or as an opportunity, as the young artist did. I believe that God gives us challenges from time to time just to let us practice our choice of reaction. When we come face-to-face with a huge obstacle, our choice will tell the world which kind of person we have chosen to be, a defeated negative person or an overcomer. It is a choice that we get to make. It is the choice that we make when those little everyday problems come our way, the ones that will prepare us for the big challenges of life that all of us will one day come face-to-face with.

As you read this book, you will find some misspelled words, some grammatical errors, perhaps some wrong dates, and some personal opinions. Try to remember that this is my autobiography, the way I remember the story of my life.

That is why I believe that writing my autobiography is important. Consider, if you will, that it is being reminded of the victories that gives me confidence to attack situations with the belief that victory will be achieved. As you read this story of my life, you will find that several chapters are filled with challenges. Some of which are potholes in the road that I have traveled in my more than eighty-five years. Others, however, have been boulders.

You will find that I have been truly blessed and that I consider my greatest possessions to be my family. And you will read about why seeing or hearing from my children every day is so important to me. This book was written more for me than anyone else. I am constantly reminded that God has blessed me beyond measure. My desire is to honor him and live my life pleasing in his sight. It makes me *feel good . . . all the time.*

Chapter 2

My Early Years

I was born a middle child in a family of fifteen children on March 21, 1937, at 8:05 p.m. Just as were many of my siblings, I was born at home. My parents had moved from the farm to 3425 Park Lake Road near Lansing. My father Glen and my mother Marguerite (Abbott) grew up on farms near Williamston. My mother, after graduating from Williamston High School, passed the required state exam and was given a teaching certificate. That fall, at the age of eighteen, she was teaching in a one-room schoolhouse. She taught for two years before she married my father and became a farmer's wife.

My father, after graduating from eight grades of education in a one-room school, started his farming career. After marrying my mother, they worked for a number of years as tenant farmers in the Williamston area. Dad thought that it was important that if he were to succeed, then they should have kids and calves every spring, calves to grow the dairy herd as well as children to help with the ever-increasing workload. For a number of years prior to my birth, they lived and worked on the Miller dairy farms just east of Eaton Rapids on Plains Road. I have heard many stories from my parents, as well as my elder siblings, about life on the farm in those times. While electric power was not available in rural areas, they did have a generator that was used to charge batteries to run the milking machines and the lights in the barn. Use of electricity in the house was limited to what was left after chores were done. It was a life of hard work and few luxuries.

By the time of that cold March evening in 1937, when I joined the family as the tenth child, we had left the farm, primarily because of the Great Depression. My father had gotten a job at the Olds Motor Works in Lansing. We lived on Parklake Road, which was, at that time, part of the Okemos School District. My father was thirty-seven years old, and my mother was thirty-five at the time of my birth. I was the tenth child in the family, all single births, during a twelve-year period. My parents had five additional children in the next seven years. These were tough times for everyone. I have, over the years, heard many stories of how the family supported one another during those difficult days. A favorite story that I have heard many times through the years is told by my third-eldest brother Wayne.

My father gave the three older boys—Robert, Russell, and Wayne—enough money to go to the movies in Downtown Lansing. Admission to the Fox Theater was 10¢. After attending the *Shoot 'Em Up* movie, starring Tom Mix, Robert realized that if they walked home instead of taking the bus, they had enough coins for two ice cream cones. So they went into the ice cream parlor and purchased the two cones. Robert then asked his two younger brothers to go around the corner to eat their ice cream so he wouldn't be tempted. Certainly, it was difficult times, such as those during the Depression years, that I believe strengthened our family. Robert's sacrifice for his younger brothers was just one of many that the family gave for one another. I personally have no recollection of the years that I lived on Parklake Road. However, I have, over the years, heard many stories about our family life during that time that we were living off the farm. It was the love of the farm, instilled in both parents at an early age, which caused them to long to once again be tillers of the soil and to enjoy the sight and sounds of life on a dairy farm.

In 1938, my uncle John Beaman, who owned several grocery stores as well as other properties in the city of Lansing, agreed to assist with financial support, helping my parents once again get back to the farm. He purchased a farm a mile north of Dansville at 537 S. Willamston Road, where the Weaver Gravel Company is now located. It had a large white farmhouse with a huge, long white barn (the barn collapsed just a few years ago from neglect). By this point in time, the two elder boys were teenagers, and Wayne was not far behind. Dad's idea of rearing his own workforce was starting to take shape. Dad also hired as a hand his eldest brother Clyde to work on this new farm. Uncle Clyde and his family lived in the house south of our house, on the curve just north of the village.

It was here on the farm that I have my earliest recollections. My dad was recognized near and far as an outstanding farmer who worked long hard hours and took good care of his milk-producing cattle. We had tractors during this time but also made good use of horses. They were used much of the time by my elder brothers to till the fields in preparation for planting and for cultivating crops as well.

I do remember several times while living there when some of my other uncles came to go pheasant-hunting. I have special memories of my uncle Kenneth. He was one of my dad's younger brothers, who lived in the city, and who loved to go hunting. I don't remember that my dad hunted, but Uncle Kenneth would take the older boys out to the fields. Rarely did they return empty-handed. It was clear that even at that early age, my personality was starting to take shape. I was a short kid with curly carrot red hair and a big smile. I also had a well-developed imagination.

It was that imagination that some people found rather amusing. For instance, someone gave me a pair of red high-top rubber boots. Now I know that I actually remember those boots. I believe the reason is my father told me never to wear them down in the lower level of the barn. That is where the bull was. Dad said the bull would chase me if he ever saw my red boots. So I used to sit on the steps going down into the milking area of the barn and watch the men doing their chores. There is one story I don't remember at all. However, I have heard it told many times. It seems that a salesman stopped by the farm. I was out playing in the yard with several brothers and sisters. The salesperson wanted to know where the boss was. As the story goes, I told him that I was the boss. According to the story, I told the salesman that my dad, my uncle, and my brothers worked for me. It has been said many times that was neither the first nor the last of the imaginary stories that I shared with anyone who would listen.

I have a faint memory of going to the Methodist church in the village with my sister Josephine and some of her girlfriends. I can also remember one day at the noon meal, hearing my mother telling my dad that the doctor was coming that afternoon to give a measles shot to all of us kids. Well, I had witnessed the men in the fall, killing the cattle and dressing them out for our winter meat. They would bring a cow into the barn, tie the hay mow rope around its hind legs, shoot it in the head, then quickly haul the cow up in the air, and cut its throat. I certainly did not want to be shot. So I ran across the road to Mrs. Stid's house, and I told her that I was going to be shot by a doctor and that I needed a place to hide. She let me sit on her cellar way steps. I felt real safe until one of my sisters came and got me. I don't remember ever getting the shot. However, I am sure that I did.

I can also remember the birth of my youngest sister Barbara. Barb, like many of us, was born at home, some not only without a doctor present, but when my mother was in the house alone, Mom would send the younger children outdoors to play and then send one of the older kids for a neighbor lady. Not only did Mrs. Stid come when Barb was born, but she also brought her scales and weighed her. Even though I was a preschooler, I have memories of living there on the farm, and most of what I remember was good. However, not all that happened while living there was good. In fact, a tragic accident occurred, one I don't remember but one that had a tremendous effect on my life and our whole family.

During those years, we were a very active farm family, with a large dairy herd and other animals as well. We were also very involved in the county 4-H farm program as a family. Not only did the elder kids have farm animals and crop exhibits at the county fair, but my parents were 4-H leaders as well. With such a large family, we did very little traveling, but people came to our house to visit us. So it was with the 4-H club. They always had their meetings at our farm home. It was after one of those evening meetings that some of the high school boys and my father were fooling around, when one of the boys got Dad in a headlock. At the time, no one knew how serious his injury was, he complained little, but it was later determined that my dad had developed a brain hemorrhage, resulting in a blot clot on his brain.

In 1942, the war was in full swing. Robert enlisted at the age of seventeen and was soon sent into battle. My parents had an opportunity to buy their own farm, 110 acres, in Bunker Hill Township. The farm was on DeCamp Road just west of Bunker Hill Center. It was and is known as the DeCamp family farm. We now had this unbelievable huge house with twelve-foot ceilings and with more than a dozen large rooms, also a large barn, with hay mows and a lower floor milking parlor as well. We also had a very large chicken coop, an important future building. One year after moving to the DeCamp farm, Russell enlisted in the army. It was about this time that we really began to understand the seriousness of my dad's problem. Every once in a while, he would go insane. His strength would allow him to overpower several people. He would become violent, trashing everything in his path. I have memories of my brother Wayne and several neighbor men holding him down until he would come back to his senses.

When Wayne enlisted into the service, my mom had to have my dad put in the mental hospital in Battle Creek. He was there for about two years and really was never the same man that he was before the 4-H club meeting experience on the Dansville farm. We sold the cattle and lived on primarily chicken and egg farming, also over the next few years grew vegetables, such as tomatoes, potatoes, and melons. My mother and elder brother George, and later Wayne when he got home from the service, sold most of this produce door-to-door in Lansing. They also sold fresh dressed chickens and fresh farm eggs to their city customers. I never got to do this, but I did on a few occasions stay at my grandparents' home in Lansing, while they were peddling their products.

When we moved to the DeCamp farm, I was five years old. I joined with my brother George and my sisters Eunice and Shirley in attending the Bunker Hill one-room school. This was a typical country school with grades one through eight in the same room. I have lots of memories of that school. It was a time of not only learning reading, writing, and arithmetic, but also a time of learning to get along with others. These were days of outdoor toilets and a potbellied stove in the center of the room for heat. In the front yard was a water pump with a big steel handle. Just south of the schoolhouse was the woodshed. It was used for storing wood and coal used to heat the schoolhouse and a place that several of us boys had to visit from time to time to select a whipping stick.

In the late fall, I was sent to school wearing a blue coat that one of my sisters had worn the winter before. A neighbor found me crying, standing beside the road. He brought me home not knowing why I wasn't in school. My dad met me at the door, turned me over his knee, and proceeded to explain in a very physical way that it was time for me to go to school wearing what I thought was a girl's coat or not. At that point, staying warm and making sure clothes were worn out from being used took precedent over style. I wore that coat the rest of that winter. I still had my carrot red curly hair that my sisters liked to curl and play with. I would put lard on it trying to make it lie down smooth and straight. Pictures of me taken at that time reveal how short I was but also that I was always wearing a smile, "feeling good" even in country school.

Life on the farm was difficult. Because of my dad's physical condition, Mom could not depend on him to supply our needs, and she decided to go back to teaching school. She got a job teaching at a one-room school, about 5 miles from our home. It was called the Bachelor School. This was the beginning of an even harder life for Mom, who worked away from home as well as being mother to the seven of us kids still at home. But I remember mostly the good times on the farm, playing with my brothers and sisters and enjoying country living. We always had lots of food to eat, most of it fresh from the farm. Sundays, we had lots of company, aunts and uncles and cousins galore; food, fun, and fellowship. I have fond memories of my aunt Treva (the wife of Kenneth, my dad's brother) playing hide-and-seek as well as kick the can. These were simpler days when toys were invented and imagined by the children that played with them. We enjoyed playing tag while climbing and walking the beams in the hay mow trying to catch one another without falling and injuring or killing ourselves.

It was at the Bunker Hill Church of the Nazarene that I first heard about Jesus. The pastor was Rev. Carl Barnes, a heavyset man with a big smile. Songs like "What a Friend We Have in Jesus" and "The Old

Rugged Cross" I learned there, and they still are two of my favorites even today, some eighty years later. That little country church, with no inside plumbing and no heat most of the time in the winter, was full of the love of Christ. As a Nazarene today, I'm not so sure those small country churches should be closed as a poor investment of our tithes and offerings. We didn't have a choir or a big organ or anyone who could play it if we did have one, but singing, praying, and preaching of God's word was done in my presence, something that I will never forget.

Also, in Downtown Bunker Hill, we had, in addition to the Nazarene church, two grocery stores and a gasoline pump. That is until one morning when we were walking to school and noticed that Herricks store, a white wood-framed building, was on fire. It burned to the ground, so Mr. Herricks bought the other store, which was across the corner. That store had the gas pump out front, so now he had the corner on; not only the grocery market, but he also owned the gas pump. It was always exciting when Mom would send to the store for flour or sugar or whatever. Mr. Herrick always gave us a stick of candy.

My childhood on the Dansville farm as well as living on the DeCamp farm in Bunker Hill were happy times indeed. Without a doubt, my very best friend in Bunker Hill was Miss Olds. Her first name was Leona. I just called her Miss Olds. She lived next door just west of our farm, and every day I would walk down to her house after school and put her cow in the barn. She worked somewhere in Jackson, and when she got home, she would let me help her feed the chickens and let me milk and feed the cow. I don't remember getting paid with money, but she liked to feed me cake and pie. Maybe that was where I got my appetite for pie. Oftentimes on the weekend, I spent the night at her house, and in the evening, after supper, we would put jigsaw puzzles together. She did not have a well at her house, so we had to take milk cans to Mr. Graham's house and fill them for drinking water. She did have a cistern in which rainwater was stored to be used later for bathing and washing laundry. She was a special lady who treated me very well. I regret that I did not spend more time with her in the last years of her life.

At that time in my life, I knew nothing of sport teams. I had never seen a television. A radio was a piece of furniture that we listen to in the living room. We listen to it to hear the farm report at noon, or in the evening after supper, we listened to the news and sometimes music. We had a coal furnace in the cellar, it heated the lower floor of the house, but there was no heat in our upstairs bedrooms. My mom cooked on a wood-burning cook stove with a water reservoir on one end. Each of us kept a house brick on the stove that we wrapped in a paper at night taking it to bed to keep our feet warm. It worked very well as I remember. That wood-burning stove in the big kitchen was where the bath water was kept warm. On Saturday night, we had to have a bath, so my mother would bring into the kitchen the laundry tub, put warm water from the cooking stove reservoir into the tub, and we got our bath, youngest first. The youngest had their bath, then stood by the open oven door to keep warm, while the next child stepped in, and so on, right up the line. I can remember my mother saying that she would wash as far up as possible and then down as possible, then I could wash possible. She just kept adding water after each bath to the tub. I wonder how we survived with little or no disinfectants, poor refrigeration, and less-than-perfect hygiene. I am not sure, however, that we were sick any more than people are today.

Without a doubt, I had a great childhood overall, a large family that cared about one another and parents that worked hard to overcome the many challenges that they faced. My brothers and sisters gave me a multitude of opportunities to learn about different personalities. That has been very helpful in assisting me in understanding and meeting the needs of customers. My parents were overcomers, especially my mom. Her example, lived before me, taught me how to react to difficult situations. I believed that this was impressed upon me at a very early age, perhaps before the age of ten. That was the age that I was when for the last time, we moved, from the farm to the city. Well, city might be an exaggeration. We moved from the DeCamp farm in Bunker Hill to the village of Dansville.

Chapter 3

The Move To The City

It was in the summer of 1947 that we moved from the farm to the city. Well, actually, we moved to Dansville, a small village of about 450 people. There were seven of us kids still living at home at that time: George, Eunice, Shirley, Jack, Jim, Larry, and Barbara. Dad got a job working for the state highway department, working on bridge construction and repair. Mom was still teaching in one-room schools. At the time of our move to the village, she was teaching at the school about 5 miles south of the village on Williamston Road. This was the last home my parents purchased, a relatively-small house compared to the one we lived in at Bunker Hill. The upstairs had just one bedroom, so the three girls slept in a bed at the top of the stairs. A curtain hung in the doorway separated them from the boys' room, which had two double beds. George and Larry slept in one, and Jim and I slept in the other. We did not have a closet, just a metal storage cabinet to hang clothes in, and a dresser that we shared. I don't believe that this was unusual for the times. We had boys' clothes and girls' clothes. Whoever got up and got dressed first dressed the best. Last guy up got what was left.

As I reflect on the years that I lived on the corner of Cook Street and Willamston Road, they were good times, times that gave me a solid foundation for "feeling good," *at play, at work, and especially at home.* We were poor, and I mean really poor. Our father worked very little, and the habit that had gripped him over the last several years caused him to drink up most of his money. Although Mom was teaching, it was in another era. Teachers were paid very little and received income only during the school year. It was during those years that I came to believe that difficult times bring out the best in people who take a positive approach in overcoming difficult situations.

In my lifetime, I have met and got to know many good people, people who have outstanding qualities, who were hard workers, who had great faith, people who understood the importance of positive thinking. Mom had all those qualities and more. I know of no one in my lifetime who overcame more difficult situations than she did. During those summers, when we had no income from my father and my mother didn't receive pay for teaching, we survived only because of Mom's determination and her resourcefulness. I remember we would pick strawberries or huckleberries or whatever was in season. Mom made it like a contest, first who could pick the most and then who could go around the village and sell the most. I did not realize at that time that was how she bought us the food that we ate. Mom, who had a positive, determined, make-it-happen outlook all her life, set an example that made an impact on my life.

I also learned the importance of saving for a rainy day. As I mentioned, Mom did not receive pay during the three summer months, and yet the bills continued. Somehow she saved enough to care for most of the summer needs. She also had a great relationship with Mr. Humphry at the Dart Bank in Mason. He knew about Mom's challenges and had confidence in her. One day in late summer, a Consumer's power truck stopped in front of our home. The driver came to the door and was clicking a pair of wire cutters. He asked for Mom. His instructions were to collect a late payment or cut off our power.

We were all frightened as kids, and I remembered my mother called and talked to Consumer's Office, which was then in Mason, then to Mr. Humphry at the bank, who called Consumer's for her. Consumer's power company called the man at our house and told him it had been taken care of. I am sure there were many other such situations that we knew nothing about, and I now understand what kind of pressure she had throughout my childhood. Saving for a rainy day may not solve all the problems, but Mom's emphasis on how important it is has been a great help for me many times in my life.

When I think of Mom, I remember how she just would not allow her children to use words like "can't" or "won't." To say "can't" always brought the response "Can't never did anything." To tell my mom that "I won't," would invariably bring the response, "Oh yes, you will." Mom just would not accept the notion of defeat as an option. The stories of what she did and how she motivated others to excel would fill a book all by themselves. Unless you lived during the era of the '50s, it will be hard to understand what she was able to accomplish. In 1950, there were seven children from the age of nine through seventeen and a husband who was sick, physically and mentally. Dad, during those next few years, was a danger to us and to himself.

I don't want to relate too much of the fear that we had of him when he would drink whiskey, but I do need to put into perspective what our home life was like. Like most people that have a problem with alcohol, Dad would be a great guy for days at a time. However, without warning, we could come home from school to find him not only intoxicated, but violent as well. I have memories of him throwing furniture at Mom, using vulgar language, and throwing his lit cigarettes around the house. Mom sometimes would stay up all night just to protect us. Of course, he would be asleep in the morning when we went to school and when Mom, without sleep, would go to school and teach. I want to point out that I believe this problem of drinking was a direct result of the injury Dad received years before. It was the blood clot in his brain that developed while wrestling with a high school boy at a 4-H meeting.

I loved my dad. He gave me a great deal of good advice, especially in the early years of my life and the later years of his life. It was those years in between that were difficult. Even during the time that alcohol controlled his life, I learned a great deal about what to do and what not to do. Certainly, after watching how he treated my mom, I was determined to always show respect to women. His conduct when I was a teen made it impossible to bring friends home. We never were sure what his condition would be, what he might say or do. However, during the last year of his life, when Dad came to California to stay with me, he was the dad that my elder brothers and sisters had told me that he used to be. I am thankful for that experience.

My fifth-grade teacher was Mrs. Crossly. She was an older experienced teacher whom I liked. My mother told me that if I made the honor roll, that she would bake me my own apple pie. I got all Bs, and I got my pie, one of the few times that I ever made the honor roll. This was a year of adjustment, moving into the village, going to a school that was so big, eating lunch that was cooked right there at the school, so many students to get to know. I did make many friends, and I did enjoy myself. It was in the spring of that school year that I turned eleven and was old enough to join the Boy Scouts of America.

That was the first of many times I went to summer Boy Scout camp. My elder brother George also went. It was the day when we got home that Mom and Dad celebrated their twenty-fifth wedding anniversary. It was a great party with my mother's parents and many aunts and uncles in attendance. The summertime was a fun time for the kids living in Dansville. We played cowboys and Indians just about every day. I was always Gene Autry, the singing cowboy; Jim was Roy Rogers; and Larry was Red Rider. We also played a lot of baseball, with every kid in town wanting to be on my sister Shirley's team. She was, without a doubt, the best ball player in town. I remember the high school basketball coach told her that if she would cut her hair, she could play on his boys' team. She was to later be named athlete of the year at Asbury College for her skills in softball and basketball.

Perhaps it was in the evening that we had the most fun. Our favorite pastime was a game called kick the can. We played this game on what was referred to as the "free show lot." This was across the street from our house. On Wednesday night, at dusk, a large cloth sheet was stretched across a wood frame, and old movies were shown. Everyone would sit on their blanket, eat popcorn, and watch old western movies that were shown after the local merchants advertising. This activity drew large crowds (these were pre-TV days), and in those days just as today, they left a lot of trash. I earned 10¢ for cleaning up the lot on Thursday morning. I usually found several coins and assorted junk in addition to earning 10¢. Long after the free shows ceased, the lot that was used during daylight hours for baseball games, and at night for kick the can, was known as the free show lot, even by kids who had never seen a show there.

My Boy Scout days started while I was finishing the fifth grade and continued uninterrupted until I was twenty-one-plus years old. It was a great experience for me, teaching me a great deal about the outdoors and getting along with others. Dansville had a very large scout troop, and for most of those years, Gary Briggs was our scoutmaster. We had our own campsite on a state-owned property about 3 miles south of the village. We called it Camp Pine Tree. It was a place that produced many good times, and it was where friends were made and developed. Some of my fondest memories were the nights we played football games under the moonlight. We also had a lot of fun harassing couples who would come out to the area to park and make out. I especially like to think about the time that we tied a car to a tree, and then about twenty of us boys rushed the car, yelling and shining our flashlights in the car windows. When the couple finally got themselves put back together enough to drive away, they left the back bumper of their car behind.

Another fun activity was the snipe hunts. Each year we would take the "rookie scouts" out at night to catch snipe, leaving them in the woods with a paper bag and a flashlight. They would shine the light into the bag and call the snipe while we were supposedly out chasing the snipe toward them. The game was to see how long it would take the rookies to figure out that there was no such thing as snipe, which were attracted to their bag because of the light they were shinning into it. I was amazed that each year we were able to play this game, and every time there were new scouts who tried to catch those snipes.

Scouting was where I was introduced to leadership, beginning by being elected assistant patrol leader. Over the years, I was selected to each leadership position, from patrol leader to senior patrol leader, to junior assistant scoutmaster. When I was seventeen, the Dansville Scout committee selected me to be Gary Briggs's assistant scoutmaster. On my eighteenth birthday, I became the youngest scoutmaster ever. It was while I was in Boy Scouts that I first realized how much that I liked being up front of people. For me, talking was easy in front of a crowd. The bigger, the better. I still enjoy it today.

It is also very important for me to share how important the people of the Free Methodist Church were in my life. When we moved into the village in the summer of 1947, on the weekend of July 4, Pastor Cummings called on us on Saturday to come to Sunday school the next day. From that point on, until I was about fifty-five years old, I attended that church. Oh, there were times when the white church (United Methodist) across the street had a contest, and I went there a few Sundays just to win a prize, but it was the Free Methodist Church that I was attracted to. Two people, Lawton Hedglen and Helen Young, had a tremendous influence on my life. Mr. Hedglen was my Sunday school teacher and oftentimes invited me to his home for a hot dog roast or just to play games with the other kids in our class. His life of non-smoking, non-alcoholic drinking, never using profanity, and always gentle and soft-spoken was something that I needed to see in a man. Lawton, along with Gary Briggs, influenced not only my lifestyle but my personality as well. Sunday school had a tremendous influence on my life, and I still consider it the most important church service of the week. I only wish that my children shared my feeling.

Helen Young lived on the corner just a block south of our house. In fact, she lived halfway between where I grew up and the first house Darlene and I bought some years later. Helen was a very special person. She lived a consistent Christian life, and her testimony affected not only my life as a young boy, but the lives of Darlene and our children as well. When I was in my middle fifties, she was still my Sunday school teacher, and she was still teaching me how to live a Christian life, with Jesus as an example and Savior. Helen's prayer life was without equal, her faith was indescribable, and her giving unmatched. She did not have many material things in this world. She believed that her treasures were in heaven. That is where she is now. It was my privilege to be able to chair a committee that raised the money and sent a group of people to build a church in the country of Haiti in her memory.

The other person who had a tremendous influence on my young life was Gary Briggs. Gary was the custodian at the school. When I was in the seventh grade, he hired me to do yard work at his home in the village. It was during those next two years that I learn how to manicure a lawn and how to edge sidewalks and to make flower beds and shrubs compliment a house. When I was in the ninth grade, Gary hired me as a student custodian at the school for 25¢ per hour.

It was during those years as a young teenager when I was in need of a man role model. Gary fit the bill. His wife was a teacher at the school, and they had one young daughter, Karen. I knew Gary as my scoutmaster. Now he was my boss. He taught me a great deal about the importance of having a good work ethic. I don't recall that he ever complained about how fast I worked. He just expected that I would do the job, whatever it was, right the first time. He was constantly showing me how to do all kinds of maintenance work, such as painting walls and refinishing wood floors. He would not tolerate people being late for work, and he expected that I would be there every day, Monday through Saturday. I can remember all too well that not only did Gary expect the job to be done right the first time, but he also demanded it. If we left a light on in our area when we were done, fine 5¢; left sweeping compound in a corner or beside a desk, fine 5¢; didn't see a cud of gum on the floor, fine 5¢. Remember, I made 25¢ per hour, and believe me, he deducted all fines from our pay. At the time, I'm sure that I wasn't very happy about losing those nickel fines, but I sure learned to check carefully my area of responsibility My brother Larry and I worked for Gary at the school until we graduated. I stayed nearly two years after graduation. I remember that my first contract called for me to work nine hours a day, Monday through Friday, and five hours on Saturday. My salary was $2,500 per year. Payday was Thursday after the third Monday of each month, and my take-home pay was $170 per month. Obviously, I didn't get rich working as a school janitor, but I did learn a great deal. Years later, when I was hired to be in charge of custodial maintenance, it was Gary Briggs, my mentor as a boy, who came to the school to give advice and counsel.

My high school years were uneventful. My goal was to graduate but not to use any more energy to get my diploma than was necessary. I enjoyed school for the fun, friends, and activities that it provided. My best friends were the four top students in our class. Not a whole lot of their intelligence rubbed off on me. Most of my energy was used to develop my skills as a custodian. It was during those years that I learned the importance of being at work every day and striving to exceed the expectations of those that I worked for. Certainly, there were a number of time that I was too sick to go to school, but I was never too sick to be at work. As I reflect on those days of sweeping floors, cleaning bathrooms, and washing windows, they were days that prepared me for future success. Perhaps the only experience that helped me more than using cleaning products was purchasing them. Twenty-five years ago, when I started selling, my past labors were of tremendous help in my successful sales career, just as my leadership responsibility in scouting was extremely valuable in the management positions that I have enjoyed.

In addition to my church and scouting activities, during my high school days, I also was very involved in class and student government. Beginning in the ninth grade, it was important to start planning our senior trip as well as developing a plan to finance it. We needed a fundraiser each year, and I was very active in selecting what it would be and making sure that it was successful. The only trophy that I ever received in high school came from the Curtiss publishing company for leading in school sales of magazines. I also was given the book *I Dare You*. This is an excellent book on achieving success by being determined and never giving up on what it is that you want to accomplish. I have put that advice to the test several times so far in my lifetime. We had a newspaper drive one year that as we collected literally tons of used newspapers, all through the year we tied them in bundles and stored them in a farmer's empty barn. In the late spring, the company we sold them to brought a semi-truck out to the barn, and our classmates loaded the bundled newspapers into the truck. It was a lot of work but very profitable for our class project. We decided that during our last days as classmates, we would travel by train together, just before graduation, to Washington DC.

For most of us, it was our first trip to our nation's capital. For me, it was the first of what would be many visits to Washington, each one special and everyone an educational and emotional experience for me. Walking up the steps inside the Washington monument, being inside the nation's Capitol Building, walking into the White House, these were but a few of the exciting things that we did while there. Several of us also went to a Washington senator's baseball game. That is the team that later moved Minnesota and was renamed the Twins. It was a great trip, and as a class, we earned enough money so that all our classmates could go, and we had money left over.

In addition to serving in a leadership role in my class, as vice president, I also was on the yearbook staff as photographer. I really enjoyed helping create our yearbook, and many of the pictures in it were ones I took. High school was obviously a very busy time for me. It was a good time, a time that I reflect on with fond memories. It was a time that prepared me to live life in a world where people have different values and seek after that, which is of no interest to me. My years as a teenager were years that I chose to have my life influenced by people of high standards: people I was convinced had tremendous faith in God, people who expressed confidence in me, people who, I believe, sincerely cared about me as a person. I am referring to Lawton Hedglen, Gary Briggs, and most of all Helen Young. These people, and many others as well, had time for me, time to tell stories about their successes as well as their failures. They shared their opinions about many of the issues of the day; not sharing what they thought that I wanted to hear, but what they believed I needed to hear. As a teenager, I oftentimes had strong ideas of what was right and what was wrong. In our high school yearbook, written under my picture was "There are two sides to every story . . . my side and the wrong side." In some ways, I guess, I haven't changed much, have I? Certainly, my personality and ethical standard was greatly influenced by those people whose names I have mentioned, and I'm thankful for having them as my mentors.

Like all children, I too grew up and became a teenager. And right on time, I became one of those who believed that I knew it all. In fact, I can remember a saying that my mother used to say to us when she thought we were feeling too big for our breeches. It went like this:

> You can tell a *freshman* by the way he eats his lunch.
> You can tell a *sophmore* by the way he carries his books.
> You can tell a *junior* by the way he looks. You can tell a *senior* . . . but you can't tell him much.

My parents were wise when I was a young child. It was while I was a teen that they seemed to have lost their wisdom. I am so glad that by the time that I became a parent, they had gotten wisdom back again. As the years go by, what they said, even while I was a teenager, seems to not only make more sense now, but I have also come to understand that it is impossible to understand your parents until you become one.

Chapter 4

My Youth, Girls, And Marriage

While I was going to country school in Bunker Hill in the 1940s, a group picture was taken of all the students attending the school. When the picture came back, there I was holding the hand of the little girl standing next to me. I believe from that time on, I knew that there was a difference between boys and girls. I have enjoyed getting to know any number of girls as most boys do, most of these were just friends, but I did have a girlfriend or two during my school days.

Church, I found out, was a good place to meet girls, and because so much of my social life took place at church activities, it made good sense to look for a girl who went to our church. When I was in the ninth grade, Rev. Harry Moore was the pastor of the Free Methodist Church where I was a regular attendee. Sunday school was the best-attended service of the week. Many children and adults who came to Sunday school did not stay for what was called in those days the after-service. Today it is referred to as the worship service, or sometimes we just call it church. Pastor Moore was trying hard to increase the size of the attendance of that little brick church. He began going out in the country and picking up children and bringing them to Sunday school. The Moores had five children of their own, and there were a number of town kids who attended as well. Because kids attract kids, Reverend

Moore had little difficulty finding a car or two filled with kids that started attending every Sunday.

Out on Clark Road, just north of M-36, there was a widow who lived alone. To supplement her income, she cared for what were called in those days wards of the court. Mrs. Stewart kept girls that the court system had removed from their parents. Normally, she had two or three girls at a time who lived with her until the court system decided who would have custody of these children. It was into this situation that a young girl by the name of Patricia Ellis was sent by the court. She and her brother were taken from their parents who at the time lived in Lansing. They were not bad people. Neither were they child abusers. They simply were trapped in a life of alcohol abuse.

When Pat first started attending Sunday school, we became friends. She was much younger than I, but at the time that did not seem to matter. Each Sunday Reverend Moore would bring her and the other girls along with as many kids he could get into his car to Sunday school, and of course, because he was the pastor, they had to stay for church as well. It wasn't long before she wanted to come to the Sunday night service and the midweek service as well. I really don't think that her desire to attend every service possible had anything to do with church. But I was certainly happy that she wanted to come because I was there for every service as well.

Writing notes during church, sitting beside each other during services, that was about all there was to our dating. I did not have a driver's license. Besides, Mrs. Stewart did not allow any of the girls who lived at her house go anywhere with boys, nor did she allow boys to come to her home. From time to time, Reverend Moore would have a party at the parsonage, and all of us kids would be together to play games and have light refreshments. Of course, I also was able to see Pat at school. However, she was never allowed to attend any school activities.

This relationship lasted off and on for about two years. Patricia's parents were given custody of her once again, so she moved back to Lansing, where she lived with her brother Roy and her parents. They lived in a rented house on North Center Street. The house was torn down several years ago, and I don't remember what the house number was. I did hitchhike to Lansing to see her a number of times during the months following her return home. It was, however, a very foreign situation for me. Mrs. Ellis seemed very nice to me, but from time to time, she would disappear for several days, only to return without explanation to where she had gone. Mr. Ellis worked at a local construction company and had a real drinking problem that seemed to occur without any reason or warning. Patricia's parents were born in Olive Hill, Kentucky, a small town in Eastern Kentucky in what was called a dry county—that is, a county where selling alcohol had been outlawed since the days of national prohibition in the 1920s. In later years, I visited Olive Hill twice, my only visits to what is called Appalachia, a very poor area of our country in the mountains of Eastern Kentucky and West Virginia.

Mr. Ellis lived in the better part of Olive Hill. It was still a very underdeveloped situation, no indoor plumbing, but his parents' house was clean and well kept. Mrs. Ellis, on the other hand, came from a house that would better be described as a shack. The house had one room that was used as kitchen, dining room, and living room, and there was also one other room used for the bedroom. Not only was there no inside bathroom—there was no any inside plumbing at all. The house was along the railroad tracks, where they picked up pieces of coal that fell from the coal cars when the freight trains went by. This was used to heat the house in a stove that sat in the middle of the living room. It has to have been the poorest home situation that I have ever seen. The town was something out of the past, with old rundown buildings and people who obviously had not ventured outside of the area during their lifetime. But they had a taxicab, a cab in a town of no more than three hundred people, in an area that covered less than a square mile. So I asked why.

One of the Patricia's uncles told me that I should find out for myself. He told me to flag down the cab, and when we started to travel to tell the driver that I needed some moonshine, so I did. When I told the cab driver what I wanted, he said to leave $5 on the car seat, which I did. He stopped the cab in front of an old hardware store and told me to go inside and come back in ten minutes. So I went into the hardware store and looked around for a few minutes, and when I went back outside, I found that the cab was there, so I got in. There on the seat was a bottle of clear liquid that I assumed was moonshine, the only liquor that I have ever bought in my life. When I got back to the house, one of the men sampled my moonshine and assured me it was the real stuff. He also said that the job of the cab driver was to distribute moonshine to the residents and visitors of Olive Hill.

Soon after Patricia moved back to Lansing to live with her parents, I went to visit her. Her dad, while in a drunken stupor, told me that she had moved to California to live with an aunt. I did not hear from her for several weeks, but she finally wrote to me to say that she was happy and safe. We wrote to each other a few times, but as time went by, so did my thought of Patricia. A new family by the name of Emerson moved to Dansville and began attending the Free Methodist Church.

This new family that started to attend our church had four children, two boys and two girls, who were excellent singers. The eldest girl was named Montel. She was attracted to me, and the feelings were mutual. Church was the center of my social life and attending youth activities such as swimming at Pleasant Lake or going to the parsonage for games and hot dog roast, and such was I as well as what most of my friends did for fun. We had good times without having to spend very much money.

In the spring of my senior year in high school, I purchased a car. It was a four-door gray 1950 Plymouth that I paid for $150 cash. I remember that I bought it from a used car dealer in Williamston. On my way back to Dansville, I stopped at the Emersons to show off a little. Montel and her younger brother and sister and I were all sitting in the car. We were listening to the radio. I was a little too proud of my car. It wasn't long before I had to keep turning up the volume so we could hear the radio. Finally, it quit altogether. The battery was dead. So there I was, my new car tied with a chain to the tractor of my girlfriend's dad, while he pulled me down the road to get it started. I did not feel quite as proud of my car then, so I just drove home.

As I have mentioned, I was working as a student custodian while in school, a job that Montel's mother thought was below what she wanted for their eldest daughter. I remember one Sunday morning when I was standing next to her singing a congregational hymn, she leaned over and said, "Why don't you just move your lips and not sing? Then no one will know how bad your singing voice is."

It was a long time before I ever sang in church again. She did all that she could do to break up our relationship, and she finally succeeded. After graduation, I decided to continue working at the school. I was devastated, heartbroken, and extremely angry with Mrs. Emerson.

The week after the breakup, I was leading our youth meeting. The meeting was being held in the large room in the lower level of our church. While standing there, focusing on the scripture that I was going to read during the service, I looked up just as Patricia walked into the room. I took her home after the evening service to Lansing where her parents lived. It was obvious that she did not want to live there. However, she had no other place to live. Less than two months later, we got married at the Dansville Free Methodist Church.

At the time that I got married, I was still working at the school in Dansville as a custodian. My salary was now $3,300 per year. We lived in Mason on Sycamore Street. I continued to work at the school until an insurance salesman, who had sold me a policy while I was still in high school, convinced me to go into insurance sales.

I went to work for the Life Insurance Company of Virginia. I was part of a branch office that was located in Downtown Lansing. I really liked selling insurance. It was my first sales position. I learned a great deal about preparation and planning; both would be of help to me in later years. The part that I liked most about the sales positions that I have had over the years has been the people I have been able to meet. In this job, it was required me to go door-to-door during the day, setting up appointments for the evening. I then would in the evening when the husband and wife were home and make my presentation. I had a number of different closes that I practiced that helped me close the sale, getting the order. I learned early in my career that I really enjoyed the challenge of selling and the feeling of success that getting the order brings.

Our first child came into this world on July 10, following our marriage the previous October 5. Of course, everyone was counting the days and months, having no way of knowing that Patricia was a virgin when we got married. I was upset having to lose my girlfriend at her mother's insistence, and Patricia just wanted someone to provide her with a safe place to live. Not the best reasons to get married, but that was the way it was. Ten months after our first child came number two. Life was moving pretty fast. Being gone every evening selling insurance was not near as exciting, and I really didn't like missing out on doing my part helping my nineteen-year-old wife with two babies.

It was when I began thinking about the changes that were taking place in my life when I became a father that caused me to think about changing careers. My brother Robert had written to me several times. He invited me to come to California and work for him in his flower shop. Patricia was excited about moving back to the state that she had enjoyed so much as a teenager. It seemed like a great opportunity, and after a few weeks of preparation, I resigned from my job at the insurance company and made plans for a westward journey

Chapter 5

Little Children . . . God's Gift

By the time that we moved to California, I had become the father of a beautiful little girl named Janet K, and then just eleven months later, God gave us what every father dreams of, a son. We named him Randy after me. However, because I didn't want him to be called junior all his life, we decided to use my middle name. After a great deal of conversation and a number of suggestions, the name Randall J was agreed upon. I didn't think that it was possible for life to get any better. To be the father of two beautiful children, what a privilege . . . It was so exciting that it wasn't long before God gave us baby Jeff as a bonus.

It was after we moved to California that Jeff joined our growing family. Patricia insisted that it was her turn to decide on a name. She did agree, however, after a number of other suggestions, to use my father's name, Glen, as Jeffrey's middle name.

These three children, from the moment of their birth, were important to me. Little did I realize, even at the time of Jeff's birth, the challenges that we would have during the first few years of their young lives. As I reflect on my life as a young person, I am so thankful for Sunday school teachers and other Christian friends, the Christians in that little brick church in Dansville who loved me and cared about me. I also am thankful for the pastors who preached the word without apology. It was at the altar in April

1955 in the Dansville Free Methodist Church that I accepted Christ as my Savior. Not only was my life changed, but also were my priorities. It was because of my relationship with Christ that I had the strength to make it through the difficulties that we faced. When these three children were all under four years of age, they would be exposed to a life of insecurity and an uncertain future. It was then that I realized a truth that has served me well: To accomplish true success, it is first necessary to determine *what is important* and *who is important*. It became very obvious to me that my children were at the top of my list. As the years have passed, other names have been added to my list of *who is important*. But my children that I believe were given to me as gifts from God will, for the rest of my life, have a special place, not only on my list but in my heart as well.

The following pages give a description of their lives, as I have known them three children who have loved me and have accepted the love that I have given them. As young children, we were inseparable. At the time they did not understand why I was so uncomfortable when they were out of my sight. They had no way of knowing about my fear, not for them, for me; a fear that I believe will be a part of my life for as long as I live. As teens, Darlene and I were so proud to be with them and to support their many activities. We enjoyed being able to discuss with them their plans for the future and long to listen as each shared with us their dreams and aspirations.

Today they are more important to me than ever. Their unannounced visits are always something that we look forward to. We don't take for granted the privilege that is ours to have all three of them living with their families close by, allowing us to spoil our grandchildren and to watch with pride as they grow up right before our eyes. As I reflect on the chapters of my life, writing chapters that share about the "exciting times" have been the most enjoyable. Those are the chapters about the experiences that we have had since Darlene came into our lives and got involved with our children and grandchildren, chapters that are about our lives together. I have been reminded and refreshed that these are the people who have helped me, as well as many others to keep what is important to me, and to remember every day who is it that is really important in my life and to be able to say that I FEEL GOOD . . . ALL THE TIME.

Chapter 6

My Little Girl Janet

Janet K. Cook came into our world on July 10, 1958. Born in Mason, Michigan, at what was called the old Mason hospital. It was a three-story brick building located on East Ash Street just east of the United Methodist Church. When we brought her home from the hospital, it was to an upstairs apartment located at 128 W. Sycamore Street. We later moved to Dansville to a house that I rented from Paul Hedglen, just kitty-cornered across the street from my patents. To say that Janet was a beautiful baby would be an understatement. I'm not sure where she got all her good looks, but I am sure where she got her personality. She just could never lay still, sit still, stand still, or be still. She was born talking and giving directions on how she wanted everything done. In her early years, we moved a lot. We moved from Dansville to Mason, living in an apartment over the Ingham County News, the building that is now part of Kean's. That is where we lived when her brother was born, when she was just eleven months old. We named him Randall J. From Downtown Mason, we moved to a house on Harper Road just east of College Road. I was able to plant a large garden, and we also had a nice big yard. It was while we were living there that the invitation from my brother to come to California was extended to me. We packed up our two children and headed west to Hawthorne, California.

When we got to Robert's, he helped us find an apartment in nearby Inglewood. Bob owned a flower shop on Westerner Avenue at 45th Street in Los Angeles. He had encouraged me to come out to California where the weather was always sunny and warm and there were lots of good jobs. Getting a job was easy for me; I was soon hired by a furniture company that specialized in building baby furniture the first week we arrived. Two months later, we moved to a house just down the street from our apartment. It was part of a six-house complex that was owned by a widow named Mrs. Mills. By the time Janet was seventeen months old, she was living in her seventh home. It was there that her youngest brother Jeffrey joined our family. She was thirty-three months old. Six months later, Janet and her two brothers became part of a single-parent family. I was the single parent.

As big sister and the only lady in the house, she became a "can I help?" kind of child. In those early days, I tried so hard to make her look nice, making sure she was wearing a clean dress, that her hair was brushed, and she had on the right colored socks to match her dress. Even in those days, Janet was helpful, knowing better than I what looked best with what. Perhaps some of those early experiences are what we see in our Janet today. She always looks so well-groomed and properly dressed. Janet is a compassionate, gentle, beautiful person and is always ready to help everyone. She is still and will always be *my little girl*.

I believe Janet's life really began as did her younger brothers when Darlene came into their lives. Oh, I can remember good times, bad times, but mostly hard times during the first five years of her life. Janet was almost five years old when we moved back to Dansville, to that pink house I rented a block from the school, on the corner of M-36 and Adams Street. We were back home where I felt it was safe for Janet and her brothers to go to school. I wanted them to be a part of the same Sunday school where I had learned about Jesus. Today I am thankful that she has little recollection, if any, of those days when I was striving to be mother and father. We arrived home in Dansville about the end of May, on a Wednesday. I remember that my younger brother Larry arrived home from college that same evening.

The two of us went job hunting the next day. Larry knew about a company that was installing a natural gas pipeline between two towns southwest of Jackson. They were reportedly looking for laborers to help dig ditches. Remembering how our late father told us to get a job, we got up extra early the next day, arrived at the work site fifteen minutes before the workers' starting time. We were dressed for work, having our lunch pail in our hands. The job foreman was really impressed. He hired us on the spot, telling us to report for work on Monday morning. We were to be paid $2.50 per hour as long as it didn't rain. That was $100 a week before taxes. Known as the gold dust twins by the other pipe line workers, we had a great summer. As the summer passed, Janet made a number of friends mostly at church, namely Cindy Sawyer, Linda Young, and Naomi Barnett.

Soon it was time for school to start. Janet was privileged to have Martha Glynn as her kindergarten teacher. That was an exciting year for Janet; she loved school and was always excited about coming home each day and sharing with her brothers what she had learned. Mrs. Glynn told me that she was a good helper and a joy to have in class.

If I remember correctly, when she was just a baby, I heard a loud noise coming from her room one night. When I went in, she was jumping up and down. She continued to do that until she was about thirty years old, I think. I knew before she was old enough to walk that she would someday be a cheerleader. I was right. My most vivid memories of her as a young girl were her motherly instincts. She was always concerned about her younger brothers and was a great help to me in caring for them.

On June 13, the summer after she completed kindergarten, Janet and her brothers and I joined with Darlene Marie Collier to become a family, a family that God has blessed beyond measure.

When we were planning our life together, we wanted to make the transition smooth for our children. We decided to rent a house a few miles from Dansville; we wanted to have a little space while we were adjusting to each other. We moved into a retired Free Methodist pastor's home on Noble Road near Williamston. It was permissible in those days for teachers to bring their children to school with them when they were living outside the district where they were teaching. So Darlene took Janet and Randy to school with her each morning.

We lived in Reverend Anderson's house for the next two years; they were good years for my little girl. She quickly adjusted to Darlene, and what has been a beautiful relationship began. I think that like her brothers, she liked not having to be taken to a babysitter each morning when I went to work. She made friends with the kids who lived next door, and all five children played well together.

A lifelong friend, Helen Young, told Darlene and me one night after church that she believed that God wanted us to have a house that was for sale in Dansville. She believed it so strongly that she loaned us $500 for the down payment. It was the first home that we owned, paying $8,000 for the 115-year-old house. It had a large yard and was only two blocks from the school, church, and just about everything else in Dansville.

Janet continued to be a very active child. Playing with the Stone kids who lived next door, as well as the many other kids who lived in our neighborhood, it was obvious to all that Janet was a very happy little girl. She played from daylight 'til dark. Never was she still for a minute. She was very active in our church, enjoying CYC, Bible school and church camp. She also enjoyed the many camping trips that we went on with our secondhand Nimrod pop-up camper.

We had a policy to teach them financial responsibility, or maybe we were just not very affluent. Anyway, we gave each of them a few dollars to spend as they saw fit when we went on our camping vacations. On one of those many trips, Janet, who was extremely frugal when it came time to spending her money, well, it was her turn to buy pop for the family. So during a pit stop, which it seemed to me she and her mother needed far too often, she decided that each of us didn't need a whole bottle, so she bought two bottles for us to share. We all still kid her about that even today. In reality, she is very generous with all she possesses, but at the same time, I think she still is frugal. I believe that some of those experiences when she was young helped her later in life when she two found herself needing to stretch each available dollar. Perhaps making decisions at a young age of deciding when and where to spend her money helped at least a little.

When we purchased the house in Dansville, each of the children got their own room. Jeff might dispute that his room was at the head of the stairs, and Janet and all her friends had to walk through his room to get to her room. When they grew a little older, Janet and Randy switched rooms. That helped a little, but Jeff, just because he was the youngest, believed that he got a raw deal.

My memories of Janet, as she prepared to enter high her school years, were of my little girl starting to look like and act like a young lady. Some of her interests were changing. Even though she was still active in the church, the band was becoming a focal point in her life. She worked very diligently at perfecting her skill at playing the French horn. Our high school band director was having a good influence on her life, helping develop her leadership skills. In high school, as she had been all her life, I would describe her as a bouncy teenager, not only as a cheerleader, but also in everything she was involved in. The enthusiasm of the moment, regardless of what project had her attention, gave Janet reason to give it her very best. We were privileged to follow her around the state as she competed in French horn competitions. I might mention here that I could not believe that anyone could come out of a bedroom in the condition of Janet's, looking so beautiful, so neat, and so well-dressed.

Janet was a very popular student, serving her classmates in a number of capacities. As a section leader in the band, president of the student council, and holding a number of other offices, it seemed like she was always busy planning or implementing some new programs. She liked running track, setting several school records. I remember the year that she ran boys' cross-country because they did not offer any program for girls. She even ran in the league boys meet. She didn't finish last either.

Janet did have boyfriends, all nice guys and other details you will have to get from her. I will say that she always had them pick her up at our house, and they always came inside to meet me and visit for a few minutes before she went out with them. We never had a curfew, believing that our trust in our children was far better than any rule having to do with time.

After high school, Janet decided that she wanted to be a court reporter. The summer after high school, she worked in a doctor's office in East Lansing to earn money for college. She enrolled in Lansing

Community College (LCC) that fall. A few weeks into school, she decided that college just wasn't for her, at least at that time. One of the greatest privileges that a father can have is to walk his daughter down the aisle of a church on her wedding day. I had that privilege, and she was a beautiful bride. I am sorry that the marriage didn't work out and that it caused her a great deal of pain.

We are thankful for the two grandsons who are very special boys. They have brought a great deal of joy into our lives. I had no idea how much I would enjoy being a grandfather. It is a name that I never tire of hearing, especially when it is one of our grandchildren who is calling me. I remember the time when they were living in a manufactured home in Mason Manner Park. Janet and Chris were baking cookies; he was just a toddler at the time. While Janet was taking a cookie sheet out of the oven, Chris crabbed on the hot oven rack, burning his little tender hand. I received Janet's phone call only to hear that the flesh was falling off his hand. I drove as quickly as I could to their home. His hand, even though it was only skin that looked like it was falling off, sure looked bad to me. We went to Lansing, to the ready care, and they took care of his badly-burned hand. I never let the phone ring without answering it like I had a habit of doing before that episode with Chris's burn. Janet has done an excellent job of rearing her boys, and we are very proud of them.

As the years went by, one constant that remained in Janet's life was her employment at Felpausch Food Stores. Over the years, she was given many promotions, tremendous responsibility, and way too many hours away from home. As I look back over those years, perhaps the job was good for her. It kept her steady, busy, and tired.

The past couple of years have been very good to Janet. Once again, she has regained that bounce that has been her trademark. Darlene and I believe that the reason for this positive change in Janet has been certainly, in part at the least, Brian, who has done so much for her and for the boys, not only providing them with a beautiful home just around the corner from where we live, but also stability in many areas of their lives. Chris has told us many times that he believes that Brian is the most intelligent person he has ever met.

I have been very pleased in the interest that Janet has shown in caring for their large yard and flowerbeds. The pond, new trees, and the country field that they have made into lawn are things that they can be proud of. Oh, it is great to have a daughter like Janet for our very own. I am sure that everyone who knows her would agree with me that she is reason for her dad to FEEL GOOD . . . EVEN AT WORK.

Chapter 7

Randall J

Born on June 23, 1958, in the "new" Mason general hospital located at 800 East Columbia Street in Mason, Randy, our first son, joined his sister in my growing family. At the time of Randy's birth, Janet was only eleven months old, just a baby herself. We were living at the time in an apartment upstairs over what was then the Ingham County News. It is now part of Kean's store. I was selling life and health insurance for the Life Insurance Company of Virginia. We soon moved to a house at 3165 W. Harper Road just east of College Road. However, it wasn't long before Patricia and I decided that we should move to California.

Randy, from before he could even walk, has stood beside me in good and challenging times. Certainly, he also had to overcome, as did his brother and sister, the loss of his birth mother. Randy was just two years old when she deserted us. These, I am sure, were difficult times for a young boy. Even though he has told me that he has no recollection at all of his life before Darlene, I'm sure there are scars. When we were living in California, Randy really enjoyed the outdoors. In the months just before the car struck us, Randy spent every minute he was allowed riding his tricycle and soaking up the warm California sunshine. His smile, personality, and leadership skills were already starting to take shape as strong assets.

Randy and I were involved in an accident when he was two years old. We were crossing the street when a car struck us. You can find the details of this crisis in chapter 9, but let me record here that even though Randy does not remember it, I do. I believe that as a parent, each time we do something special for one of our children, there are rewards. As I have thought back over the years about those lonely days and night sitting beside his hospital bed, pleading with God not to take him from me, I learned to never take my children for granted. The love and prayers, which I invested in that young boy's life during those difficult days, have been returned to me many times over. Certainly, I believe that it was God who gave our children to us. He gave me strength as I sat feeling helpless beside his hospital bed. And it was God who answered my prayers for Randy. But I realize that I am the one who has received the biggest blessing. Randy has been and is very special to me. He is much more than a son, and he is a trusted friend. The promises that I made sitting there in that hospital, I have tried my best to keep. It has been easy, and the benefits are ongoing.

If I could describe Randy's life while we were living in California, it would be a happy little boy with a big smile, who always looked up at me squinting his left eye, believing that whatever it was that I had just said must be right. Randy, just like his younger brother Jeff, looked to his sister Janet as a mother figure. Randy always wanted to confirm that whatever it was that he wanted to do or wherever he wanted to go was okay with Janet.

The trip home to Michigan from California was uneventful. Like his brother and sister, Randy was more cooperative that anyone could ever believe. I can remember one rather humorous experience; Jeff was thirsty and was riding in the back seat with Janet and Randy. Seat belts, at that point in time, had not yet been invented. I had a gallon thermos of milk in the front seat next to the potty chair. I didn't want to stop more than what was absolutely necessary. The top of the thermos was also the cup. Randy got Jeff a cup of milk. I was driving along, paying little attention, until I heard Jeff say, "All gone." I looked back quickly just in time to see the cup bouncing down the road as Jeff threw it out the window. We had never even heard of air-conditioned cars. Well, I didn't turn around and retrieve the cup, but I did have to stop at a store and buy one. That perhaps was the only incident that I remember that slowed down our trip home, except for the time that I turned the wrong way coming out of a truck stop on Route 66 between St. Louis and Chicago that cost us about two hours of driving time. However, that was entirely my fault.

When we arrived in Michigan at the end of May 1963, Randy and Jeff would stay during the day with Mrs. Call. Janet was enrolled in Mrs. Glenn's kindergarten class and joined them during the afternoon. At that time, Mrs. Call lived about a block north of the little pink house that we lived in. She was a wonderful Christian lady who continued to be a part of their lives for the next several years. I would feed the kids breakfast in the morning and then take them to her home. Janet would walk to school and back to her house. Mrs. Call was a soft-spoken lady, whose personality was what all three of the children needed during those days of their young lives.

For Randy, just as for his brother and sister, the days just ahead were going to change his life for the better, a change that would impact the rest of his life. During the year before he started school, he met and began to get acquainted with Darlene, mostly at church and church activities. I really can't remember any specific time or incident that happened between them. However, Randy needed to have a mother, and she was, as he would later state, "all mother that he needed."

On June 13, 1964, Darlene and I were married, and Randy had the mother that he needed. She would have a lifelong influence on not only his growing-up years, but also be an example for him as he made his choice of a profession as well. As I wrote earlier, Randy has told me many times that he remembers very little of his life before Darlene. I believe there are good reasons for that; certainly, he has focused on the happier time of his young life.

The early years of Randy's education were years of just "having fun." Certainly, to say that he didn't take school seriously would be an understatement. I believe that his goal in his early elementary days was to make people laugh. However, let me point out that I don't remember that he ever got in trouble. He just had fun, like the time he convinced David Sprout, his young friend, to jump off his table, pretending that he was Superman when he was in the second-grade classroom of Mrs. Akers just as she walked back into the room. For Randy, teacher conferences were always exciting; we would hear what a nice boy he was and how happy he seemed to be all the time. There was not a lot of time spent telling us how well he was doing academically. But I believe that every teacher really enjoyed having him as a student.

During his junior high years, Randy did not have a lot of interest in his personal appearance. In fact, it was a time in his life that he thought that the only time he should comb his hair was when he went to church. Clean well-pressed clothes were not seen very often on Randy when he went to school during that time in his life. However, it was during those years when two very important traits first appeared in Randy.

They were his work ethic and his understanding of the importance of tithing his earnings. Because Darlene and I recognized Randy's energy level, we decided that I needed to keep him tired out. I decided to get him interested in lawn mowing, and together, we got him a job mowing at least one lawn per day, Monday through Friday. This kept me busy repairing the mower, but it was worth the investment. Randy still has the same desire today as he did when he was twelve years old: making a lawn look as good as possible all the time. I believe that the training that Randy got from mowing lawns, as well as working at the school, paid off. His work ethic has served him well. He also should never forget how God has blessed him for his hard work and his living in obedience, which includes tithing.

It was also during junior high school that Randy got interested in the band. He started out playing the trumpet, an instrument that he continued to improve on throughout his school career. The band and Jon Francis were good for Randy. During high school, it was the band that helped keep him interested in school. And it was the band that gave him a stage to perform on, and perform he did. He traveled as did Janet and Jeff with the Dansville High School Band to performances around the state and across the country and were contributors to the band's many successes. The band also gave him opportunity to develop his leadership skills and hone his competitiveness.

It was during the middle part of his junior year in high school, with the help of his uncle Larry, that Randy decided to become an elementary schoolteacher like his mother. This was a real turning point in Randy's life; it gave him the motivation that he needed to make dramatic improvements academically as well as in his appearance. It also provided the direction that he needed to begin putting his priorities in place. Certainly, he would never be able to excel in school like Jeff, nor would he ever develop the personality of Janet, but by just being focused on his strengths, by just being Randy, he would succeed in achieving his goals. When Randy walked across the stage on graduation day, he did so with a great deal of pride. He likes to tell people that he graduated number six in his class. When pressed, he acknowledges that their names were called alphabetically. His name was read sixth. Darlene and I were pleased to see him in his cap and gown walking across that stage. Whether he finished first or last, he finished.

It must have been during his high school years that Randy read Tom Sawyer. He decided that he could emulate him to his own advantage. I never cease to be amazed at how he got underclassmen in the band to take his trumpet home and polish it and believe that it was their privilege to do so. I actually heard boys washing his car in our driveway, when he was at work at the school, say how excited they were that they got to wash Randy Cook's car. He was practicing this skill, getting children to want to do well rather than trying to make them. This has helped Randy become an outstanding principal, motivating children and teachers in the Jackson School System.

Randy decided to attend LCC during his first two years of college and then to transfer to Michigan State. While at LCC, he lived at home with us on the farm east of Dansville. During the summer, after his second year in college, he got a job as a summer replacement at Oldsmobile. This was a good job, almost too good. The pay was high, and the workload was light, and my fears were that he would stay right there. But Randy had decided what his goal was; he was not going to be denied.

It was his determination being a teacher that caused him to decide after graduation to move to San Antonio, Texas. I was devastated. For the first time in the lives of my three children, one of them was away from me. And yet at the same time, we were proud of Randy for going where the jobs were. Now, Randy could prepare himself

Feeling Good

to fulfill his dream of becoming a teacher, like his mother and his grandmother as well. While in Texas, Randy continued his college education taking classes at the University of Texas preparing himself to earn his Master's Degree in School Administration. He received that degree after returning to Michigan and getting a teaching position in Jackson. Soon, another desire of his heart would come true—becoming a dad.

The year after purchasing their first home in Mason, Justin came into his life, and after, oh, so long, at last, they were parents. Justin certainly was a gift from heaven. We were so happy. Justin arrived by way of an adoption agency called Christian Cradle. We were excited for Randy and to have a third grandson. In 1990, Randy did what seemed impossible to me. He got a new job (building principal), a new home, and a new baby (Mallory) all in the same year. Now, that is what I would call a stressful year. What a joy Justin is. His smile and gentle personality have warmed the hearts of many people. Mallory, our second granddaughter, started her young life by having colic and cried for the first six months. I don't think I've heard her cry since. Her enthusiasm and bounce remind me so much of her aunt Janet.

Randy's popularity continued to grow receiving promotion after promotion in the Jackson school district. He was appointed to both of the large elementary schools in the Jackson system. The superintendent said that he was their best principal, so he had to move him to where the biggest challenge was. After several years as principal at Frost Elementary, he was assigned to care for another small school as well as serve at the central office in charge of various other responsibilities. The Jackson Schools paid him for the extra work, but we believed that it was taking a toll on his health.

When Kelly came into our family, I think Justin said it best when he said he had never seen his dad so happy at any time during the nineteen years of his life. Kelly has three grown sons who have become part of our family, and they have been given a new lease on life. It's so good to once again see Randy with a sparkle in his eye and a spring in his step. Kelly has made him into a new man.

In Randy's lifetime, he has succeeded in a number of ways, not only as a caring son, brother, husband, and father, but as a professional as well. Not only was he named teacher of the year for the entire state of Texas his first year of teaching after receiving his master's degree from MSU, but he was also promoted to the position of building principal in the Jackson City Schools in 1996. Since that time, Randy has won the educator of the year in his district as well as the Milken Award given to outstanding educators after a national search for the best teachers and building administrators. It came with a beautiful trophy and a check for $25,000. In the spring of 2007, Randy was selected as superintendent of Springport Schools.

As Darlene and I are remising about Randy and his life, I can't help but think of those early years and remember all the trauma that he and his brother and sister had to overcome. Just to think of all that he has accomplished in his fifty-plus years, to say we are proud of what he is, as well as who he is, would not really express how wonderful we feel. Randy is still always close by, especially when I need some help. I cannot remember a day in the last few years that he has not called me or stopped by. He certainly has given me many reasons to BE FEELING GOOD . . . ALL THE TIME.

Chapter 8

Jeffrey Glenn

Born on May 6, 1961, at Rosewood Hospital in Los Angeles, California, Jeff was the third child born into our family, a pleasant surprise. Just like his elder brother and sister, he has been and is a joyous addition to the family. I didn't what any of my sons to be called junior, so Randall, my middle name, and Glen, my father's middle name, enabled me to continue our family surnames without the junior stigma. It was perhaps more difficult for Jeff than for Janet and Randy to have been left in the first year of his life without a mother. I was especially sensitive to this during those difficult times. It was during that time that he was so dependent on me for his care, that he developed insecurities, which I believe he has to deal with even today. From my earliest memories of Jeff as a young boy until today, now a husband, father, and police officer, Jeff has always been and is a gentle, compassionate, caring person.

As a baby, he was pretty lively and kept me busy trying to care for him. This was especially true when after the car hit Randy and me and I had my right arm and hand in a cast for several months. I recall that it was very difficult to put the top on his baby bottle tight enough so it would not leak. Those days were long before Pampers. I had to use cloth diapers and safety pins. To change him, I would lay him down crossways on the bed, pin one side, run around the bed and try to pin the other side, before he rolled over. I remember that during the time, my father was with us. Whenever he came into the house, Jeff would be totally his. He gave my dad a lot of love, and my father returned it by caring for him, feeding him, and even on a few occasions, changing his diaper. That is something that my mom told me later years that my dad never did for any of his own children.

During those years in California, and the first year after we moved back to Michigan, Janet did a lot of mothering. She would always call him Baby Jeff, a name that has stuck with him all his life. When Randy and Janet share stories about him, they still often refer to him, when he is not around, as Baby Jeff. I remember that Janet always liked to comb his hair and take him for rides in his stroller. It was Janet who seemed to always be beside him wherever he was. She would help me at night by rocking him to sleep. Oftentimes it was Janet or Randy who would lie down beside him in his bed and sing or play with him until he fell asleep. I needed that time to iron and to mend their clothes. Although Janet and Randy undoubtedly suffered through those days that I was striving to be mother and father, it was Jeff, I'm sure, who had the most difficulty.

When we made the long trip home from California, Jeff was a gem. He really seemed to enjoy the trip and, like his sister and brother, never really gave me any challenges. However, after we returned to Michigan, he became very attached to me, literally. I carried him wherever we went those first few weeks. It was okay with me. I have wanted all our children to stay close. Believe me, I haven't changed. Having the privilege of being the father of three beautiful, healthy, well-mannered children was something that I didn't take for granted. For as long as I live, they will always be my children.

I believe, although he probably was too young to remember, June 13, 1964, was one of the most important dates in his life. When Darlene came into his life, everything changed for my youngest son. I married Darlene because we were in love. I wanted her for my wife forever. My children were in need of a mother who would not only love them, but also care for them. This was definitely an important consideration in deciding to marry Darlene. They were no longer my children. They soon became our children. Jeff certainly, over these many years, has benefited from and responded to Darlene's love, as have his siblings.

When Jeff started school, his goal was to learn to read. He loved to be read to by anyone, often carrying around a book and handing it to anyone who would read it to him. When he came home from kindergarten after his first day of school, he was upset that he had not been taught to read. His interest in reading I think came from the amount of time that Darlene, Janet, Randy, and I read to him in those preschool years. Well, he did learn to read, and read he did. In fact, he read everything he could find.

It was not long before we realized that not only did he love to read, but he also had an incredible ability to comprehend what he read. This has continued through not only in elementary, high school, and college, but throughout his life. Today in his late 40s, Jeff still enjoys reading, and the knowledge that he has retained still to this day amazes me. However, reading and comprehension were not his only skill that we saw early in his life.

It was evident that he had a special gift of eye-to-hand coordination, something that would allow him to have successes in a number of areas. It was while he and I were lying out in the yard when we lived in the village, and he was shooting hickory nuts off the big tree at the back of the yard that I was first made aware of this skill. This talent continued to develop as the years went by, not only in sports, but also later in life. Jeff is now a sharpshooter as a policeman. This became evident in school as he started playing sports.

Jeff's basketball career started when he was in the seventh grade. It ended when he graduated from high school. In between, there were lots of stories to share, stories about his success as a shooting guard and stories about overcoming injuries. One of my favorites was his nine-for-nine shooting from downtown in a game at Williamston during his senior year. We still have an article from the paper in which the Williamston coach expresses his disbelief that anyone could shoot that well from that distance. Jeff had a number of games that he led his team to victory, none more exciting to me than a game at Stockbridge. I remember that after he missed his first two shots, the coach took him out of the game. That in itself was unusual. He rarely ever missed a single minute of a game. After just a few seconds, back in he went. For the rest of the game, he didn't miss a single shot and had scored 32 points in the game. With less than a minute left in the game and a 1-point lead, the home crowd was rooting the Panthers on. Stockbridge had the ball out of bounds under Aggies basket. Taking the inbound pass, their star guard dribbled the ball off his foot and out of bounds. Dansville took a time out. Everyone that followed Aggie basketball knew what would happen next. We had seen this play so many times. Jeff curled under the basket while Chris Magsig posted up, setting a screen. Jeff and the ball arrived at the same time. A little jump shot from 10 feet, victory right. Well, Stockbridge knew the play as well. They decided to foul him hard and made him make the two free throws to win the game. He made the first shot, nothing but net. When the official gave Jeff the ball for his second free throw to win the game, an Aggie player noticed one of the Panther guys under their basket. Just as Jeff prepared to drop the winning free throw into the hoop, the defense-minded Aggie sprinted down the court. Jeff made the free throw. It was waved off because the Dansville player had left the line after Jeff was given the basketball. We won the game in overtime anyway.

I'm sure that I could write a book just about Jeff's basketball-playing days. However, that is really what they were, playing days. As a senior in high school, after many post-game one-on-one talks, Jeff decided that when he started college, he would focus on getting the best grades possible and let competitive sports be a good memory. He began his college days at Lansing Community College, following in his brother's footsteps. Jeff, just like Randy, continued to live at home with us on the farm east of Dansville.

After finishing two years at LCC, Jeff transferred to Ferris State, where he got his degree in criminal justice. Jeff finished his college career, graduating with highest honors, and prepared to start his lifelong dream as a policeman. We were proud of his accomplishments as a student, and we were excited for him as he began his career.

Jeff got his first job working in the Ingham County jail as a turnkey, not exactly what he wanted to do. However, it was only a short time later that he was hired to be a part of the Delhi Township police department

Feeling Good

as a road patrol officer. It was his dream come true. Jeff continued to live with us. We redesigned the lower level of our home into his multiroom quarters, room for his drums, a living room, and a bedroom as well. It was during this time that Glenda would become an important part of his life.

Jeff and Glenda interestingly met at a wedding rehearsal, where Glenda was the bridesmaid and Jeff was the best man. They began dating soon after, and their relationship continued to develop. They were married at the Mason Church of the Nazarene on Saturday, April 11, 1987. They began their life together living in the duplex that Jeff had purchased on East Danville Road, 3 miles east of Mason. On September 22, 1989, Glenda gave birth to our first granddaughter Jennifer Lynn. She came into Jeff and Glenda's lives and brought them joy beyond measure and was joined in 1991 by Thomas Jack, our youngest grandchild. Tommy and Jenny have brought to Darlene and me reasons to rejoice and to be proud grandparents. Jeff and his family give me reason to FEEL GOOD . . . ALL THE TIME.

In 1990, when the Delhi department merged with the Ingham County Sheriff's Department, Jeff was promoted to detective, a job that he not only seemed to enjoy but also a job that he excelled at. While working as a detective, Jeff was assigned to the Tri-county Metro narcotics Squad, a position that we found to be very scary and certainly dangerous. It was while assigned to tri-County that Jeff was named officer of the year. In his career, he has won nearly fifty awards and citations, including awards from mothers against drunk driving and a Meritorious Service Award from the US Department of Justice. Two years ago, he was promoted to lieutenant, and after severing the department as jail administrator, he recently was given control of the road patrol throughout the county. Jeff has had a successful life, educated, gainfully employed, and married to a wonderful woman, who not only has been and is a great wife but also an extraordinary mother. Having two beautiful children, Jeff and Glenda are currently experiencing the privileges and satisfaction of being parents. They currently live in the house next door. They are great neighbors, mowing our lawn and letting us borrow a cup of sugar now and then.

When I reflect on that little six-month-old baby that, as a single parent, I was responsible for rearing, I feel good about who he has become. Certainly, Janet and Randy had a very positive influence on Jeff's life, but it was Darlene who gave him what only a mother can give—a mother's love. But I believe that Jeff also is successful because he has found that hard work and striving for perfection creates opportunities. It has been Jeff's desire to take advantage of the opportunities that has assisted him in achieving success. Jeff has continued to use the skill as a drummer that he learned in high school band playing every Sunday at the Lansing South Church of the Nazarene. Today, as a successful grown man, he is my friend, my trusted advisor, and the husband and father of three people who have joined him in giving Darlene and me indescribable joy. Jeffrey Glenn is why I FEEL GOOD . . . ALL THE TIME.

Chapter 9

I'm So Grateful For God's Grace

When we moved to California, Janet and Randy were just babies. It was in the fall of 1960, when we sold all that we had, which wasn't much, and headed west. Upon arriving in Los Angeles, we stayed with my eldest brother Robert, who had been encouraging us to come to California for several months. My first task was to find a place for us to live and to get a good job. They fell into place very quickly. Just about a mile from where Robert lived in Hawthorn, we found a nice apartment on Hawthorn Boulevard. I went to work in Robert's flower shop that was located at Western Boulevard and 45th Street. A few days later, I read an ad in the help-wanted section of the paper. It was for a company that manufactured baby and youth furniture. I was interviewed and hired the same day. I would learn as the months went by that these people were to become very important to me. Even after I went to work for Babyline, I still worked in the flower shop on weekends and holidays—a job that I really enjoyed.

My little brother Jim, who was a marine, was at that time stationed at Camp Pendleton, about four hours south of Los Angeles. Jim was to become a brother that I would soon feel indebted to for the rest of my life. My parents were stilling living in Dansville. Mom was teaching first grade at the Alaiedon Elementary School in the Mason School

District. By this time in his life, my father's health was failing. He was retired and was drawing his Social Security. In 1960, thirteen of the fifteen children in our family were still living and doing well. Three of us were living in California. In the order as I can remember them, Russell was married and living in Holt; Wayne and Rose were living near Willamston; Jodie, in Lansing; Eunice, in Lansing with Shirley who was teaching school at that time in the Lansing School District; George, who falls between Eunice and Shirley, was living in New York with his wife Arlene; Linda, in Lansing; and Sandra, who fits in between Jim and I, lived at that time in Dexter. The two youngest of the clan, Larry and Barbara, were attending school, preparing to become teachers, at Asbury College in Kentucky.

Just a few weeks after we moved into that apartment in Inglewood, California, on Hawthorn Boulevard, a lady offered us free rent, if I would agree to become the caretaker of the five houses that she owned. These houses were all grouped together and were just three blocks away on the same street where were we living in Inglewood. I took the job. We moved into a nice two-bedroom home with a sun porch and a small fenced-in backyard. I also thought that it was neat to have our own palm tree in the front yard. The decision to accept this opportunity that Mrs. Mills gave to me and enabling us to have little house was truly a divine gift as I was soon to learn.

My job at the factory was really neat. Of the four hundred or so employees, no more than fifty were citizens of the United States. That was not unusual in Southern California. Many factories hired Mexicans who had green cards to do assembly work. Babyline Furniture not only hired a lot of card-carrying Mexicans, but they also hired many people they called wetbacks. These were people who came across the border, found their way north to the very large community of Spanish-speaking people living in East Los Angeles. I learned this some months after I began working there.

I remember it was just before lunch, just a few days before I had been promoted to line leader, when the assembly foreman, Jake Gregg, came to me and said, "The Feds are here."

What happened next was really interesting to me. They had brought several buses with them. They blocked off all the exits in the plant.

Feeling Good

They then went from person to person, asking for their identification. All the wetbacks calmly walked out and got on the buses, laughing and talking in Spanish. As I stood there, watching all this take place, Jake came up to me and said these guys come in here every year or two and take all the wetbacks back to Mexico. Within a couple of weeks, most of these guys will be back.

Well, Jake was right. The company didn't even hire replacements; they waited to see who was going to return to work from Mexico. Within a week, some of the people who worked on my line were back; within a month, almost all of them had returned. As time went on, I got acquainted with several of the guys, and they seemed to enjoy trying to teach me Spanish. What little I learned I soon forgot.

Soon after the episode of the immigration department's visit, the company vice president offered me a promotion to supervisor. I stayed in the same department working on the baby crib production line. I was excited for the opportunity and for the pay increase. Jake and his brother Tucker, who had befriended me since I was first hired, congratulated me. They were from Tennessee, I mean rural Tennessee. They were a lot of fun, and as the months went by, they became very important people in my life.

A few months before the birth of our second son, Patricia told me that her dad wanted to come and live with us. For the past several years, he had lived with his sister in a small town north of San Francisco. He had called and told Patricia that his sister had asked him to leave and that he had no place to stay. I really liked him as a person. He was born in Olive Hill, Kentucky, a small town in one of the few dry counties in the eastern part of the state. That is where he met his wife, Stella. During the two times I was there, it was filled with welfare families that were really poor. I always considered him a kind man; he had a good sense of humor and had always treated me with a great deal of respect. However, as a young man, Roy had a real problem with moonshine, and when he moved to Lansing, he turned to whiskey. He would go for months and never drink a drop, and then without warning, he would buy a bottle and drink continuously until he would become deathly sick. Then the cycle would start over again. Knowing this, I still agreed that it would be okay for him to come. I'm glad that I did. He would play an important role in my life and the lives of our children in just a few months.

On May 6, 1961, Jeffrey Glen Cook came into our lives. He was born at Rose Hospital in Los Angeles in the early morning hours. By now, you realize that I came from a large family. That is just one of the many privileges in my life that I have enjoyed. I never even dreamed of being the father of fifteen children like my own father was. However, I was excited about having a third child. When Jeff came home to join our growing family, he brought and is still bringing joy that is indescribable to me and our family. As I look back on his young life, I am reminded that it was God's grace that was there for us. Even then his all-knowing plan was in place. I just wasn't prepared for what lay ahead for my three babies and me.

The summer passed quickly. We enjoyed the beautiful California weather, and I especially appreciated the flowers and the many parks in the region. My job was going well. The Jewish family that owned Babyline Furniture treated all their employees with better-than-average wages and good fringe benefits. I really never realized that because so many employees were not citizens (the wetbacks). They undoubtedly paid little or no income taxes or Social Security for them. I was enjoying our home; Mrs. Mill's was very generous in providing me with materials that I needed, such as paint and wallpaper, to redecorate to our liking. Life was good, the kids were healthy, and Patricia liked her job at the airport, and then without warning, my life was turned upside down.

I arrived home from work one afternoon to find a note, simply saying, "I've had enough of being tied down, I want to be free."

Roy, who had been watching the children while we were at work, simply said, "She's gone."

I was shocked. I didn't realize that she was so unhappy. Neither did I know that she was not enjoying being a parent to our three beautiful children. I expected that the next day she would be back. However, she had, in our nearly five years of marriage, never done anything similar to this before. I tried to stay calm, not telling anyone at work or in the neighborhood about her leaving. As the days passed, I started to feel panicky. There I was, thousands of miles from home and family, with three children aged six months, two, and three years of age, and with a father-in-law who had a history of being more than a little undependable as my only babysitter. As the days turned into weeks, my fears increased. I was extremely concerned that Roy, who was being very supportive, would go on a drinking spree without warning as he had done so many times before. I knew that it was extremely important that I keep my job, so I decided to seek out a different caretaker. I asked around work if anyone knew of anyone whom I might hire. One of the ladies at work told me that her daughter might be interested. She lived about halfway between our home and my workplace. She had two young children of her own and was looking for some extra income and was excited about the opportunity of caring for Jeff, Randy, and Janet. She asked me to feed them breakfast before they came and to bring a fresh gallon of milk each day that they were there. Feeling comfortable that she was an answer to prayer, I hired her. By this time, I had heard from the few people who knew about my challenge, more advice than I really needed.

Perhaps I was a little overconfident about how well things were going, or perhaps I just wanted everything to go well, and I was unable to see there was a problem. Regardless, I was facing what was soon to become the most difficult years of my life and the lives of my three children. Sometimes people tell you more than you need to hear, such as "Jack, what you need to know is that Patricia will be back for her kids. No mother would ever leave her kids for very long."

And then I was told, "She probably will come and get them while you are at work."

As I lay awake that night, I was overcome with fear, fear that defies description. What was happening to my life? My wife was gone, I don't know why or where, and now I am being told that my babies will be gone as well.

As I woke the next morning, I believe, for the very first time since Pat had left, I got mad. I just didn't think that life was fair. I could not understand what I had done to deserve this. I decided that morning that no one was going to just come and take my children from me. I got them up, dressed them, fed them, and got myself ready for work. I decided to have a good talk that morning with the sitter.

As we left the house that morning, I decided to take a different route to her home, something that I did each day. When I carried baby

Jeff in that morning, I broke down, and through my tears, I told this young mother my situation, that I was a single parent and that I really didn't understand it or know how long it would last. She had never seen Patricia, and I explained that she was to let no one take the children, not even their mother. I shared that I really didn't even want her to let them play outside in the yard unless she was with them. I have no doubt she felt my pain. I was sure she understood my fear of losing my children. She assured me my kids would be safe in her home, that I should go to work and be confident they would be right there when I came to get them. I felt a lot better. I believed they would be safe with her.

And that was the way things stayed. I would get them up, dress them, feed them breakfast, take a gallon of fresh milk, drive around different routes with one eye watching the rearview mirror to the babysitter's. I would go to work, leave the plant, drive down different streets to the babysitter's, pick up the kids, and drive home. Once home, my plan was to never, never let them out of my sight. When we got home, I would keep them inside, while I fixed dinner. After dinner, we would go out in the yard to play. The houses behind us were connected to the street by sidewalk only. These were the homes that I was to care for. There were several young children who lived in these homes, and Janet and Randy enjoyed playing with them. I just joined in and stayed right with them, carrying Jeff around on my right hip. Mrs. Mills at this time still did not know that I was alone with the three kids. However, it did not take long for her to find out.

Next door to us on Hawthorn Boulevard lived an older couple, a real sweet lady who was always coming over and bringing the kids cookies and looking everything and everyone over. She was always asking questions; she seemed to me to be more than just a little nosy. Her husband was still selling a little real estate and caring for some rental properties that they owned. It wasn't long before the kids told her that their mother had gone away, and over she came. She immediately offered to help in any way she could. However, I was concerned that she might report to some social agency that there were three kids under four living next door to her without a mother in the house. Remember, this was in the early '60s, long before woman's lib or equal rights. I knew that I could face even another challenge: the government's need to make sure that children were being properly cared for.

I once again was about to have another tough night after a long day, which started off with the usual busy morning. Just imagine what it was like getting these three babies ready to leave with me as I went to work each day. I then spent the day working at the factory before picking up the kids, and then it was home again. Fixing dinner for us was the best part of the day. I liked to cook, and preparing a nice meal for us was relaxing. Most evenings I read to them until they fell asleep. However, my day was not done. I still needed to do laundry, iron clothes, clean house, and do the dinner dishes. I was so busy that I certainly did not have time to feel sorry for myself.

It was during these days that I, for the first time, was very thankful that my mother insisted that all her sons needed to know how to cook, bake, and do laundry. Remember that this was during the time of washing machines with wringers. I had to hang the clothes outdoors to dry on clotheslines, except during rainy days. Then I used a clothes rack in the living room. Nights after the children were asleep, the housework was done, and I readied myself for bed was when loneliness would set in. It was after I had pillowed my head that if I didn't fall to sleep immediately, I would lie there and worry, and often the tears flowed uncontrollably. Now I had a new worry—would someone see the kids dirty? Would they wonder if they were being properly fed? I thought up all kinds of reasons that I could be reported to social services. After an especially restless night, I decided that I would go next door and visit these neighbors and tell them as much as I knew. I wanted them to know what I was doing to care for my children. The next night right after dinner I dressed up the three kids and went next door to face the music.

We were very well received. I am not sure, but I don't think I told them anything that they did not already know. They assured me that they would do anything they could to help me. I sure felt better. We walked back to our house, and just as we entered the house, the phone rang. It was Mrs. Mills, and she wanted to know if I could still care for her properties. I am sure that our neighbors had called her as soon as we left. I assured her that I still wanted to care for the houses and that I really needed the help financially, and she was fine with that. Still, there was a growing fear within, a fear that just wouldn't go away. What was going to happen to the children? Who would take them away from me? When would it happen? And what would I do if someone did?

The weeks went by. We heard nothing from Patricia. The lady next door told me a friend of hers said she knew she was living not far away. She said she saw a picture in her room of the three children when she was doing some cleaning. I received this news with mixed emotions. She might come back, or she might just come and take the kids. It was late November on a very warm Sunday afternoon, while Jeffrey was sleeping and Janet was in her room playing, that Randy and I walked down to the store, which was just across the street, to buy some popsicles. A car struck us as we crossed the street in the crosswalk.

I entitled this chapter I'm so grateful for *God's grace*. As I look back upon those days, I am absolutely convinced that it was only by God's grace that I survived and, more importantly, that my children survived. On that clear, warm November Sunday afternoon, Randy and I were walking back from the store. We were walking in the crosswalk that was just across our home. He was holding on to my hand as was his custom. A car driven by a young man making a left hand turn approached the crosswalk. He did not see us. He told the police he was watching a girl walking down the sidewalk.

As I saw the car, at first, I assumed that it would stop. When I realized that the car was not stopping, I remember putting my hand on the hood, trying to stop it. At the same time, I could feel Randy's hand slipping out of mine, and then I was flying. I landed some 30 feet down the street. As I tried to get up, my right wrist gave way, and I dropped down on my face. Striving once more to get up and find my little boy, I managed to look back toward the car. The first thing that I saw was his shoe lying in the street under the car. I then saw his crumpled little body lying under the car near the rear wheel. At last, I managed to get to my feet. Having taught first aid as a Boy Scoutmaster, I knew that he should not be moved. However, he was my little boy, so I crawled under that car and took him into my arms, and as I got out from under that car, I realized that he was seriously injured.

I walked over to a bus stop bench and laid Randy down. I was trying to get a dime out of my right pocket with my left hand, not an easy task. I needed to call my brother to come and be with Janet and Jeff. Just then, the barber who cuts my hair came out of his shop. He recognized me and offered to take us to the hospital. Not one person standing or driving down Hawthorn Boulevard offered to help me. That was not unusual I was soon to learn. No one wanted to get personally involved in anyone's accident. The barber got his car and drove Randy and I down the street just a few blocks to the hospital. They did not ask me for any identification or an insurance card. They just took my little boy and me into the emergency room and began to look at his injuries. It was determined that he had a skull fracture and a brain concussion as well as a broken arm. Why us, Lord? Why us?

My brother Jim, who was in town from the marine base near San Diego, immediately went to stay with Janet and Jeff. Robert and his wife came to the hospital. It was going to be a long night. The hospitals in those days, like most buildings, did not have air conditioning, and it was hot. They brought Randy into a room, where they had told me to wait. It was very difficult for me not to pass out when I saw him, which is what I usually do when I see someone I love hurt or injured. What I saw was a sight that would be etched on my mind for the rest of my life. The hair on the right side, including his scalp, was all gone. His head was so swollen that there was no indentation between his ear and his head. His face, legs, and arms were all scratched and cut, and his left arm was broken and in a soft cast. The doctor told me that the next few hours would tell us about the seriousness of his injuries.

As I sat there by his bed, the doctors reminded me that I needed to have my injuries tended to also. That was when I first realized that my right arm was cut and bruised and my wrist was very swollen. While I had some other scrapes and cuts, none of them appeared to be very serious. By that time, Robert and his wife had gone home. They said that Jim would spend the night at my house, taking care of the other two kids. I decided not to leave Randy alone, so I sat by his bed in the hot room, trying to keep him as comfortable as possible with cool washcloths. Once every thirty minutes, I was able to give him some ice chips on his tongue. He was so hot, and he just didn't understand why he hurt so much. Because of the head injuries, they did not give him any medication for pain. Also, the doctor told me not let him fall asleep.

By eight o'clock the next morning, they felt that Randy was out of danger, but they brought some forms for me to sign, which said that I had refused treatment. By this time, Jim was there and made me have my arm X-rayed. It was no surprise that that my right wrist was broken. What was surprising is that it took almost five months for it to heal well enough to have the cast removed.

At least I did not have to worry at that time about someone taking my children from me while I was at work. For the next five months, I would be staying home, caring for them myself. That was the good news. What we would live on was another matter. Let me add here that pride is not good, even if the intentions are. I just did not want to share my problems with anyone.

Because I was employed, there was an income provision that would provide us with enough money to live on, which would come from the state. At this time, I was especially grateful for the job of caretaker of Mrs. Mills's properties so that we had free rent. After a couple of weeks, I called the office that would be sending me my check, and I was told that it would probably take another few days. A week later, I called again. All the money that I had saved, hiding it under the mattress, was long gone. I was told that I should be receiving a check any day.

There are some things that just stick in my mind, never to be forgotten. What transpired in the life of my family next is one of those unforgettable experiences. The next Wednesday morning, I had not received the check promised to me some three weeks before. So I placed a phone call to the state agency that was handling my case. I found out, while being transferred from person to person, trying to find the actual person who was handling my case (what has changed in the last forty years?), I was told that she was in San Diego. When I finally reached her in person, after some thirty minutes of phone conversations and transfers, this kind lady said to me, "Let me check your file."

A few moments later, she was back on the line. I will never forget her comment to me. "Mr. Cook, our records show that we owe you several checks, and I will make sure that we get at least one on its way to you by the first of the week."

That was not what I needed to hear. We had no money. Worse yet, we had no food. Let me confess at this time that because of my pride, or just because all my life I had been trained to work out my own problems, I had not conveyed my financial situation to anyone, not even to my brothers living in California. Regardless of whatever success I achieve in life, or whatever difficulties I face, I will never forget those next few hours. Next week was a lifetime away for us, no money, no food, nowhere to turn. Well, I did call Catholic Social Services, but they told me that because I was eligible for income from my disability, they could not help me.

That Wednesday evening, I remember putting Janet and Randy to bed without any dinner, and then I put some sugar and water in Jeff's bottle and rocked him to sleep. After they were asleep, I went outside and sat on the front steps of our home, just trying to decide what to do next. Without a doubt, this was the lowest point in my life. Not only were my children asleep with their little stomachs empty, we had no promises of a brighter future. Their mother, I had come to accept, had not only deserted me, but her three children as well. I sat there thinking about how I could accept the fact of a person, a husband or wife, leaving for another person. However, it was something else for me to accept the fact of how bad a person I really was. My wife wanted to "be free," as Patricia wrote in her note that day, and she was willing to desert her own flesh and blood just to get away from me.

I sat there on our steps for a long time, my self-esteem totally shattered, my self-confidence that I could care for my children far below empty. I do remember that I promised myself that no one would ever take them from me. I tried to tell myself that someday I would be able to give them all they needed. I promised those sleeping children I would give my life to them completely, without exception. I then asked God to shed his grace upon us, to put his arms of protection around us, and to keep us together forever and forever. I promised to do my part. I would never allow anyone to come between us or separate us from one another.

That next morning not only did the sun come up, but also the mailman came. My mom, who at this time had little knowledge of our plight, wrote me a letter and enclosed a $20 bill. That was the largest, most valuable $20 that I had ever seen or would ever have. Good times were on their way. My God had not only heard my prayers, but he also had answered them. There could be no mistaking that God was in control. That Christmas, I had $8 to spend. That was okay. I managed to talk a Christmas tree lot salesperson on Christmas Eve to give me a tree that had not yet been sold. I used the $8 to buy lots of 5¢ toys and some candy. I remember sitting there that night telling myself someday I would make up for these meager gifts. We had a good Christmas that year and every year since 1962. With the help of Darlene, I have tried to make each Christmas extra special. God has been so good to us.

I had really dodged a bullet. The checks started to arrive from my disability, and while we certainly were not rich, we had food to eat and our needs met. My father took a Greyhound bus from Dansville to stay with me and help me with the children, as well as to try and boost my self-esteem. It was quite a challenge to learn to keep house with one hand, my left hand no less. When the doctor put the cast on my wrist, he made it fit so that my thumb was unable to touch my fingers. This left me with some real problems, like putting the top on Jeff's baby bottle. Ironing and changing dippers were the most difficult to do. But as I recall, these challenges were conquered one at a time by just figuring out ways of doing what needed to be done. I began to feel much better about life and about our future. My father left for home, knowing that he had been a real help to me and, more importantly, a great encourager. It was the last time that I saw him alive.

When I was finally able to have the cast removed and return to work, I was starting to feel much better. I had heard nothing from Patricia, and life was starting to fall into a pattern, even if it was very exhausting for me. I continued to take the children to the same lady and keep the same routine of trying to keep the kids' whereabouts a secret while I was at work. I was keeping house, giving baths, doing the laundry, and shopping, as well as taking care of the maintenance needs of Mrs. Mills's properties. At the same time, I was trying to be the best dad that I could.

By this time, it was common knowledge at work that I was a single parent. From time to time, I would get this unbelievable feeling of fear, fear that something was wrong at the babysitter's. I would get into my car and drive toward where they were staying. I can remember that I would strain my eyes trying to see them while I was still blocks away. Once I saw them, I was fine, and I would return to work. But the fear of Patricia or some social agency taking my children from me was always on my mind. Once again, God provided a way, a way that I would have never even dreamed of.

As I have mentioned earlier in this chapter, the family that owned the company where I worked treated me very well. Not only by promotions and pay increases, but they also seemed to know and concerned about my situation at home. I was called to the office by the president.

It seems that I had become a topic of conversation at one of the management meetings when the company's legal counsel was present. The attorneys said that they could help relieve some of my fears by getting me legal custody of my three children. The company said that they would take care of the cost. The company president had me come to the office and meet with their lawyer, where I was given instructions on what I needed to do. The plan was to file divorce proceedings on the grounds of the soldiers and sailors desertion act of the state of California. The attorney told me that he would have to hire a detective to find Patricia and that when they got close to locating her, she would probably call. I was to give her no information, except a phone number for her to call. It was just a few days until she called. She asked me what I was trying to do to her. All I said was you need to call this number.

It was about a week later that the attorney contacted me at work. He told me that Patricia had agreed to have him represent us in court and that she had signed away her right to the custody of our children. He said that he would let me know when we needed to appear in court. This just sounded too good to be true. Why would she give up custody without even a fight? Well, the attorney had an opinion, one that I have come to accept. When she was working at the airport, she must have gotten involved with someone who did not know she was married. As the relationship developed, she never acknowledged her children, and soon she needed to make a decision between her family and her lover, and the family lost.

When I received the call telling me of the court date, the lawyer also said that the judge wanted me to bring the children with me to the courtroom. Oh my, was I ever nervous. Not only about what was about to happen to us, but also how would three little preschool children respond to being in a place like a courtroom with all these people they did not know? I was nervous over the next few days. When the day arrived, I cleaned them up and put on their new outfits, complete with new shoes. But I knew it was not going to be clothes or shoes the judge was interested in. It was the welfare of my three young children.

As we arrived at the courthouse in Downtown Los Angeles that morning, I was, as could be expected, very nervous. Nervous not only about what decisions were going to be made that day, but also, as a young father, I just was uncertain how my little children would respond to what was about to happen. When we got inside the courthouse, our attorney met us and ushered us into the empty courtroom. I remember it seemed so cold and barren. Every sound seemed to be magnified and echoed throughout the room. I thought, what if Jeff cries or Janet and Randy start horsing around as young children sometimes do? What will all these people think? Surprisingly, the only people in the courtroom were the judge, his stenographer, my attorney, the three children, and myself. The judge immediately attempted to put us at ease with a warm smile and a gentle touch. He spoke to each of the children, asking each one their name. As he took his seat behind the bench, the fear that swept over me was overwhelming. The attorney said very little, except to read the request, asking that I be granted a divorce on the grounds of desertion and that I be given full custody of the children, with no visitation rights to their mother. The judge busied himself for the next few minutes looking at the papers on the desk before him. He then looked toward us and said, "I want to talk to the two older children in my chambers."

As the judge, his stenographer, and my two children began walking toward the door leading to the judge's chambers, I could barely breathe. It seemed like they were gone for a very long time. However, I doubt that it was more than just a few minutes.

As the judge settled himself behind the bench, he looked over toward me, and he said some very nice things to me as well as about me. The judge then said, "I am granting the petition of divorce as was requested. Also, I am granting full and complete custody of Janet,

Randall, and Jeffrey Cook to their father Jack R. Cook as has been agreed upon by both parents."

This was an unbelievable moment for me. My heart was beating so loud that I was sure that everyone in the room could hear it. I was so excited to think that for the first time in what seemed like such a very long time, I would no longer need to be afraid to take them to a sitter while I was at work or to let them play in our yard alone.

As I sat there in that courtroom, a place that I really did not want to be, I was being given relief from my greatest fear, and then the judge said, "However . . ."

This day had begun with apprehension, wondering not only what was going to happen to us, but also how the children would react to being in a courtroom, with people they had never seen before. Well, they certainly exceeded my expectations. I could hardly believe what was happening to us. My worries were going to be over. Then the judge, without even looking up, said a word that will have a special meaning for me for years to come. He said, "*However*, should Patricia petition this court and demonstrate that she has settled down and ask for custody of her children, this court has no choice but to return these three children to their natural birth mother."

It was not until we had left the courtroom and the attorney was explaining to me what total custody meant, that I asked him about the possibility that she might change her mind. He said that based on what Patricia had told him when she had come to his office and signed over all rights to the custody of our children to me, that he would bet his career that I would never hear from her again. Even then, it just seemed impossible to me. How could a mother just leave and forget her own flesh and blood? It has now been more than forty years since that day in the courtroom in California. I still do not understand it. *However*, I believe that while I may never understand, I am thankful that God not only has cared for our needs over these many years, but he has blessed us as well.

As we left that courthouse with what I wanted, legal custody of my children, I was still very uneasy; I did not feel at peace. Perhaps it was too easy, or maybe it was because I had been so afraid for so long. Maybe it was because of those long evenings, when the children were in bed asleep and it was so quiet. It was then that I felt so alone with no one to talk to, and I would think about losing my babies. Regardless of the reason, there is no doubt that was when I became a worrier. I believe that from that day forward, there became a part of me that for the rest of my life has caused me to be afraid that I might lose my children. But that day, the day in court, was a day of victory. I did feel that we were ready to live our lives without fear.

Perhaps the second-best thing that happened that day in the California courtroom, in addition to having legal custody, was to realize how important my three children were to me. Even so, I soon had to accept the fact that no matter how much I loved them, how well that I cared for them, each day could be the last day that they would be with me.

That day there also was created within me a fear that was to live with me for the next twelve years. Sometimes it was the ringing of the phone, or a knock at the door, or a car driving into our driveway, or perhaps when I looked at the mail, the fear would surface. Night after night, I would get up just to see if my children were safely asleep in their own beds. The fear that the court would take away custody from me and give it to Patricia was always there. How would it happen? When would it happen? What would we do? *I needed God's grace. I wanted him to watch over us, to protect us, to keep us together.*

Certainly, it was a time that I had my priorities in their proper place; material things, who won the ballgame, or what the weather was going to be tomorrow were nothing as important to me as having a thankful heart to enjoy the real blessings of life. God had blessed me with three children. He also gave to me the responsibility of caring for them and loving them. My goal was to fulfill my responsibility.

Chapter 10

My Special Angel

I was feeding the children, getting them ready to take to the sitter's early Wednesday morning, March 14, 1963. The phone rang. It was my brother Wayne. I just knew that it was going to be bad news. Wayne shared with me that our father had died during the night from complications while having surgery to relieve him from a blood clot that had developed following a heart attack earlier that day. Dad was sixty-two years old. He had been disabled with heart problems for several years. I hung up the phone and for just a few moments, just sat there, reminiscing about the time that he had spent with the children and me, during the time that my arm was in a cast, just the year before. I will always remember how much I enjoyed the time being together with him and the all the attention that he gave my children during those difficult times. My brother Robert and I decided that we would fly back to Michigan for the funeral.

It was on the day of our flight to Michigan that, for the only time in my memory, I was with all my twelve brothers and sisters on the same day (I had previously lost two siblings). Our sister Sandra, who lived in Chicago, met us at the airport. She was about to give birth to her second child, and her doctor would not allow her to travel. Later in the day the rest of the family gathered at our parents' home in Dansville, on the corner of Cook and Jackson Streets. My father had named our street soon after we moved to the village. It was when the village got their fire truck, and the council decided that if they needed to go to a fire, they would need an address and street name. So my dad, who was an original member of the fire department, just wrote Cook on our street on the village map. The name is still there.

It was still cold and snowy during the three days that Robert and I were in Dansville. I remember walking around the village, thinking about all the fun I had as a young boy and as a teenager as well. We had moved from the farm into the village in 1949 when I was in fifth grade. It seemed so quiet and peaceful there compared to the hustle and bustle of California. While I was home, I had a chance to see by brothers and sisters. I was especially excited to visit with my younger brothers Jim and Larry, to spend time with my mom, and to once again see old friends. It was a long flight back to California, but I was excited to get home to be with my children and to return to work.

I had not been back from Dansville very long when I realized that I was soon to face another challenge. Janet's fifth birthday would soon be here, and she would be going to school that fall. One warm evening in April, I took the kids for a walk. I decided to see where the school she would be attending was. It was a scary experience. I discovered that she would be required to cross several busy streets and would have to walk some ten blocks to get to the nearest elementary school. My mind was once again filled with fear. How could I possibly expect her to get back and forth to school safely every day? Even though the court had relieved my mind of the fear that my children would be snatched from me, I still feared that I could lose them at any time by an order of the court should Patricia meet the courts requirements. Making sure that they were properly cared for and safe was always on my mind. That night I had a vision.

The Bible says that old men have dreams and young men see visions. Well, in 1963, I was a young man. That night I had a vision. I dreamed that we moved back to Dansville to live. In my dream, we rented the house of Mrs. Hefty (she was my sixth-grade teacher), which was located on south street behind the school. In fact, when Janet stepped off the front porch, she would be in the elementary school playground.

The dream got better and better. The first time I took Janet to school to meet her kindergarten teacher, the teacher was impressed at what a beautiful little girl Janet was. As she visited with her, she took a good look at me and immediately realized where Janet received her good looks. In my dream, this young kindergarten teacher would fall in love with me and agree not only to become my wife, knowing that she would need to be the mother of my three children. When I woke that April morning, I was not only *feeling good*, I was ready to head for Michigan.

Even today I believe that the job I had in California was one of the best jobs that I have ever had. Not only did I enjoy the work, the people, and the satisfaction of building beautiful products, but also the people I worked for were very good to me. However, then as now, nothing could compete with what was best for my family, and I believed that Janet would be safer if she were to go to school in Dansville. I gave my two-week notice and began to develop my plan to get ready to go home to Dansville.

I got two large boxes from work and packed some of our possessions and shipped them to Michigan. Also, I put a sign in the front yard announcing our moving sale. Two weeks later, I was ready to load our 1955 Chevrolet with some clothes and "lots of stuff." I leveled the back seat by using books, boxes, and blankets so that the kids would have room to play. I placed a potty chair in the front passenger seat so that I would not have to stop so often and bought a gallon thermos to keep milk cold, and we were on our way.

I drove to Amarillo, Texas, where we spent the night. The next morning I was just so excited that we were going home, and so with three little children as my only company, I was on my way. When we arrived in St. Louis, Missouri, that night it was about nine o'clock, and it was raining. Because the kids were asleep, I just kept driving on, too excited to sleep. About midnight, feeling a little sleepy, I decided to get a cup of coffee to help keep me awake. I was driving north toward Chicago on Route 66. I noticed there was a truck stop on both sides of the road, so I drove in, left the kids asleep in the locked car ran inside, got a cup of coffee, and I was ready to keep on driving for home. The problem was I couldn't remember whether I had stopped at the truck stop on the right or on left side of the road. I took a guess and as I headed down the highway that dark rainy night. I was uncertain whether we were headed north toward Chicago or going south back toward St. Louis. It was nearly an hour later when I realized I was headed in the wrong direction.

Heading the wrong way where I left the truck stop was the only trouble that we really had on that long journey home. Then as now I knew that God was with us, before us, as our guide, and that he kept us safe throughout the long, long journey home. *I was feeling good.* I continued driving, just too excite to stop. I just wanted to get home. I can hardly imagine driving that many miles with a one-year-old baby in diapers, a three-year-old boy, and a little girl who was two months from her fifth birthday. It was, however, an uneventful experience; one that I hope will never have to be repeated. We arrived in Dansville about noon the following day, having driven nonstop from Amarillo, Texas.

As I drove into the village, I headed down South Jackson Street, passed Cook Street, to South Street. Turning right, I headed for Mrs. Hefty's house. When I drove into the driveway, the house was gone. I was in the teacher's parking lot that was next to the playground. I sat there with tears streaming down my cheeks, and I said, "God, this can't be. What about my dream?"

I drove slowly back down South Street to Grove Street, turned left, went one block north to Adams Street, turned left, drove by the front of the school, and continued past the school to the stop sign at M-36. As I sat on the corner, I was looking right at a little pink house with a "for rent" sign in the window. I wrote down the phone number and went to my mom's house. I called. Mr. Weldon answered the phone. I knew him, and he knew me. I rented the house. I was home again. That night my brother Larry arrived home from Asbury College with his teaching degree. Good things were starting to happen.

The next day we spent resting from our long trip, introducing the children to grandma, aunts, and uncles, and helping them understand that those wide sidewalks were really streets and that they just couldn't play out there. I knew that I was going to need to get some furniture for our new home, so we went to a secondhand store in Leslie and bought two beds for $3 each. The store owner threw in the mattresses free. I bought a really neat metal drop leaf table with chairs for $5. A wringer washing machine also cost me $5. By the end of the day, I was ready to start keeping house with my three children in our home in Dansville. The two boys had a bedroom that they shared, Janet had a little room of her very own off the kitchen, and I slept on the couch in the living room.

On Friday morning, Larry and I were up early. We needed a job. Larry knew of a company that was installing natural gas pipelines between the cities of Hanover and Horton southwest of Jackson. Larry and I got to the construction site about fifteen minutes before the boss arrived, dressed for work, with our lunch pails in our hand. That was the way our dad taught us to look for a job. The boss was impressed and hired us on the spot, telling us to be back on Monday ready to work. The pay was $2.50 per hour as long as it didn't rain. I worked there for the rest of the summer. Money was a little tight, with our rent at $25 a week, and the sitter, Mrs. Call, charged me also $25 per week. For a full week on the ditch line, I received $83 take-home pay. Needless to say, we didn't have many luxuries, but I sure was happy to be home. We were also welcomed back by our church members and friends.

That summer, while working with Larry on the ditch line, we had lots of time to talk. One topic was that a teacher was coming that fall to begin her teaching career in Dansville. She had already agreed to teach a Sunday school class at the Free Methodist Church, our church. I knew that she must be the girl of my dreams, the young lady who brought me home from California. It wasn't long before I began to tell people that she was going to marry me. I didn't even know her name, but I was sure that God was sending her to me straight from heaven, *an angel* to watch over and care for my three children and me.

The Sunday before school started, I was at the front door of the church, greeting people as they came in, and suddenly, there she was. I knew as soon as I saw her that she was my *special angel*. I introduced myself and showed her to her classroom, giving her a welcome pin, which she still has in a scrapbook.

The next few months were some of the happiest of my life. While I like to kid her about how she chased me until she caught me, in reality, she was scared to death. People were telling her what I had told them about how I was going to marry her long before we had even met, and I had. There was just no way that I could be denied. I courted her in every possible way that I could think of. I'm sure that she knew early on how serious I was. We had our first date, a progressive dinner, on November 23. In the following weeks, Darlene and I spent countless hours talking about our future. There was never any doubt that we would marry in my mind, and the only question was when. As Darlene had the opportunity to interact with the children, I'm sure she realized that she would have some real challenges. They literally clung to me when I was around them. I continually carried Jeff on my right hip, Randy would walk along hanging on to my pant leg, and Janet would be holding my other hand. Our insecurity was pretty obvious. The love and dependency we had for one another was unmatchable.

We became officially engaged on Valentine's Day 1964. However, I proposed to her at the Jackson cascades in early January. Darlene was not only busy learning her career as a first year teacher, but now she also needed to plan our wedding, a wedding that not only would make her a new bride, but she also would become the instant mother of three children. As the weeks and months passed, we had many conversations about the children. She was made aware of my fear that at any time, without warning, they could be taken from me. It was during one of those conversations that I first realized how much emphasis Darlene put on her prayer life. She began praying for me and *our* children every day. After we were married, we continued that practice, and as years passed, we added each of our six grandchildren to our list. God has been so good to us and has answered so many of our petitions.

As our wedding day approached, we decided to start our life together as a family in a different home. The pink house that I lived in was way too small for our new family. More importantly, Darlene wanted to start her new life now as a wife and mother in our house. We found a nice house on Noble Road, just south of Williamston, about 8 miles north of Dansville. It was a beautiful brick house that belonged to a retired Free Methodist pastor who had been called back into the ministry. It was perfect, with three bedrooms, a full walk out finished basement, and a nice big backyard. We were thankful for a house like this as we began our life together as a family of five.

As the day of our wedding approached, Darlene was finishing her first year of teaching at Dansville; needless to say she was really busy. We were going to be married at the Charlotte Free Methodist Church, her home church. This is where Darlene grew up as a young girl and where she accepted Jesus as her Lord and Savior. She spent her teen years actively involved in the church, where a number of Christians influenced her to attend Spring Arbor College, and then on to Greenville College, where she received her teaching degree. Darlene also came from a large family (kind of large, nine kids). She lived much of her early life on the farm, moving into Charlotte when she was in elementary school. As we continued to share our plans and our dreams of our lives together, the day of the wedding was fast-approaching.

On June 13, 1964, Darlene Marie Collier became my wife. One thing that stands out in my mind was Janet running up to Darlene and asking, "Can I call you Mom now?"

The relationship that began that night has blossomed as the years have passed by, as has the mother-son relationship between Darlene, Randy, and Jeff.

We left that night for Niagara Falls, stopping at the Sunset Motel just west of Lapeer to spend our first night together. We have a receipt for the room, $8.10, including tax. We had a wonderful time, but we were looking forward to getting home and starting our life together. My sister Eunice had stayed with the children while we were gone. Before we left, we moved our furniture and clothes and stuff into our new home. As soon as we got home, we went and got our children. That first night at bedtime, Jeff announced that he didn't know where Darlene was sleeping, but he was sleeping with his dad. As we began our lives together, we were far enough from family and friends to have room to adjust to becoming a family, and yet we were close enough to visit them regularly. *God is so good*, even though the fear of losing our children was still with me every day. One night after church, a good friend, Helen Young, said to us, "Why don't you buy the Otis house that's for sale in Dansville?" It was just a block south of my mom's. We didn't think much about it because we just did not have much available cash for a down payment. Two weeks later, Mrs. Young told us that she believed that God wanted us to have that house and that she would lend us the $1,000 we would need for the down payment. The house cost us $12,000.

Moving into the village had a lot of advantages: We were just two blocks from the school, my mom's, our church, the post office. In fact, as I think about it now, in Dansville, we lived within two blocks of everything. The house that we bought was about 115 years old. It had at one time been an old farmhouse and still had a small barn. Mrs. Otis had died several years before we bought the house, so it had sat empty for some time. To say it was a little rough would be an understatement. I remember that everything inside and out was yellow trimmed in red and that it was sagging and listing in every direction at the same time. There wasn't any area of that house inside or out that I didn't rebuild during the next ten years.

As the years went by, it was exciting to see the improvements that we made inside and outside our house, as well as the renovation of our large yard. Our first house was becoming a home, a place that we spent quality time together as a family. It was there that we first had the opportunity to grow flowers. My mother was a big help. She loved flowers, and she knew how to make them grow. I remember watching her take a rose, stick it in the ground, put a fruit jar over it, and in a few weeks, she had a new rose bush. Some days I believe that if she stuck a lead pencil in the ground, it would grow. Mom suggested that we join the Dansville garden club. We were, by far, the youngest people in the club, and everyone gave us great garden tips. It was enjoyable and very educational. We also got lots of slips off their plants for us to plant in our flower gardens. We eventually had a full acre of yard where we had beautiful flowers, and we planted dozens of young trees that today are large and beautiful. This is where we lived when Janet graduated from high school. Our home there was also used on Sunday mornings for Larry's Sunday school class, and on Wednesday evenings, we entertained dozens of teens from our church.

We spent eleven very happy years in that big two-story white house at 1143 S. Jackson Street.

I got a job working at the school as the director of buildings and grounds (janitor), Darlene continued her teaching career, and our children and their friends spent many happy days playing and enjoying their first real home. But it was here that Darlene came face-to-face with Patricia for the first time. Darlene would realize how important she had become in our lives as the children decided to make their choice known, *a choice* that would impact our lives forever.

Chapter 11

Our First Home, Good Times, Great Ending

Living in Dansville had a lot of advantages for our family. With the kids being very active in school and church, it eliminated transportation problems. Darlene would oftentimes walk to school in the morning. I found that because my work required being at the school at all times of the day and night, it was nice to be living just two blocks away. During good weather, I usually rode a bike to work. As the children moved upward through the school system, they became involved in various activities. The most dominating was the band.

In a small school, scheduling classes becomes difficult. Larry shared with Darlene and me that we should make sure all three of the kids enrolled in the band. Because band was the largest class, the whole high school class schedules were being determined by it. The various sections of classes, such as English or Math, were determined by whether you were in the band or not in the band. The band teacher, Jon Francis, was a very strong disciplinarian, and as Larry put it, the band is where the good kids are.

Janet played French horn, and sure enough, most of her friends were also in the band. Not only did having her in the band affect the class sections she was in, but she also seemed to really enjoy playing and became very successful, winning various awards at district and state competitions. She was constantly battling to sit first chair and was most often successful. During her later high school years, she became a real leader within not only the band but other school organizations as well. The band was good for Janet, and Janet was good for the band. We would see her leadership in high school develop into a very successful career later in her life.

Randy decided that he wanted to play trumpet. It was a great choice. It was perhaps in the band that his gift of leadership was developed. I will never know whether he had a lot of talent or he was just determined to be the best trumpet player in the band. Perhaps it was a little of both. Regardless, Randy excelled not only in the classroom and on the playing field, but as a leader as well. I'm sure that Mr. Francis appreciated all his leadership skills. They would have a lifelong impact on Randy. It was band and his work as a student custodian that kept his interest in school. The rest of his classes were just something he had to do so that he could stay in the band.

And then there was Jeff. Starting out as a trombone player, he would follow in the footsteps of his brother and sister, well, not exactly. Jeff was his own person. He has an unquenchable thirst for knowledge and believed that the answers could be found in books. From the time that he learned to read, he was never satisfied that he had enough time to read all that he wanted. The band was where his friends were, and being in the band gave him a chance to enjoy and develop those friendships. He was placed in the high school band when he was still in the eighth grade and was moved to the percussion section. This was a decision that would benefit him not just during his high school years. Jeff did very well and is still using his high school training. He still plays his drums each week in his church. However, the band was not as important to him as it was to Janet and Randy. Jeff wanted to excel in basketball.

Darlene and I never really wanted to pressure any of our children to be anything, except to be the best that they could be at whatever they wanted to do. Janet and Jeff enjoyed athletics. Randy preferred work over play. We saw nothing wrong with either. What we did believe was that during those days of the '60s and early '70s they needed to be busy. I hired Randy to work with me at the school, originally to do lawn work and later to be a student custodian. Janet was busy cheerleading, running track, being active in student council, and eventually becoming president as a high school senior. Jeff was either reading or shooting baskets. His eye-hand coordination and his reading comprehension would be a great help to him, as later in life, he would become a sharpshooter in the Ingham County Sheriff Department.

For me, those years living in that old house in the village were years of confidence building. Owning our first home was not only an exciting and rewarding experience, but also, it was a time when I got to do things that I enjoyed. When I went to high school in Dansville back in the '50s, my favorite class was wood shop. And now for the first time in my life, I had the opportunity to put into practice some of what I had learned from Mr. Carlen, my shop teacher. I am sure that there was not a single project that did without making a mistake or two, and yet Darlene and the kids encouraged me by being excited about what I was doing to our old house.

At the time that we bought the house in Dansville in 1966, I was still working at the Fisher Body plant in Lansing. Lois Young's brother had helped me get into the shop, and I rode to work with her husband Wayne and our next-door neighbor Jerry Nowlin. It really was a good job as far as income was concerned. During those days, they could not build cars fast enough, so we were working ten hours a day and often Saturday as well. In addition to those hours, because I was trying to purchase material to use in rebuilding our house, I would oftentimes work double shifts on Fridays or Saturdays to earn extra overtime money. The job that I was hired in to do was considered the dirtiest and most undesirable job in the paint department. Not only was it extremely dirty, but it was also hot, so very hot. My job was to spray a mixture of sand and tar on the underbody of the car as they came out of the paint-drying oven. Most people stayed on that job only a few weeks and then went on the second shift to get a better job. I believed that it was important that I be home in the evenings with Darlene as she cared for our children, so in the eleven years that I worked at the plant, I never worked nights, and I never got very far from the booth. I remember well sometimes I would stay awake at night, not wanting to fall asleep. I knew that when I woke up, I would have to go back into that auto plant.

As the time passed and the children grew, our family was enjoying the best of times. We found time to go on short weekend camping trips, hauling our Nimrod pop-up camper mostly south into Ohio and Kentucky. Those were great times. They were good not only for family bonding but also for establishing rights and wrongs as the children began to reach that age at which they were seeking their own independence and making their own decisions. It was many of those times that I reflect on even now with a great many warm fuzzy feelings. We made a strong attempt to help all three become involved with the youth of the church. Our hearts' desire then and now are that we might not only enjoy our children here in this world, but also for all eternity in heaven together. We were pleased at the relationship that they had with people such as Preacher Bob and Rev. Richard Rolfe.

We also made every effort to live our own lives as an example of being *Christlike*. Only time will tell whether we did an adequate job.

I had built a backstop and ball field in our backyard. That was where the neighbor kids and Janet, Randy, and Jeff played most of the time. It seemed like the yard was always full of children. I liked it that way. They had friends to play with, and I could always be aware of where they were. At the same time, I was planting trees in our one acre yard, trees that were a little different, such as variegated maple, corkscrew willow, tulip, and gum trees. I thought that it was really neat having as many different kinds of trees that we could find. Darlene and I found a nursery south of Holland that had a lot of unusual trees. We purchased several, and they are still there growing in that yard today. I remember that I built a white board fence just behind the house, enclosing a small portion of our yard so that we could have flowers and blooming shrubs without them being trampled by all the ball players. As the children grew, it became the home run fence. And a year or two later, the fly balls were hitting the sliding glass door that went from the kitchen to our deck. I decided that our yard was no longer large enough for baseball games, so I planted a tree on home plate. An era had ended.

I still had that fear that one day there would be a knock on the door, a letter, or perhaps a phone call telling me that the California courts had decided to take my children from me. That fear surfaced every single day of their lives without exception from that October day in 1961. It was always there, always affecting my decisions on what to do and where to go. Certainly, that affected my personal life in many ways. My desire for our children did not change over the years, and it is still the same today. I wanted to be with them as much as possible, not just for them, but for me as well. During all their growing up years, I never went bowling or played golf or belonged to any organizations or clubs that would take time from them. If they were not welcome where we were invited, we simply did not go. I don't regret this in any way, for while I am sure I would have had opportunities to do other things, perhaps have even had more friends, everything in my life pales in comparison to being the father of those three little babies, babies that have grown up to be successful adults with spouses and children of their own, and yet they remain, alongside Darlene, the most important people in my life.

On May 6, 1974, Jeff celebrated his thirteenth birthday, and we were now parents of three teenagers. A few weeks later, while Darlene and I were visiting Pastor Rolfe in Port Huron, Jeff answered the telephone. The caller asked, "Do you know where your mother is?"

Over the years, we were careful to prepare our children to act responsibly should they be faced with a situation that would cause them to feel uncomfortable. Whether it was the tax assessor who came to the door and wanted to come in, or a salesperson asking personal questions, we wanted them to be able to handle any and every situation. Pastor Richard Rolfe and his wife Lois were not only our parsonage family in Dansville during those very important years of our children's lives, but we had also become very good friends. When they moved to Port Huron to minister, our family oftentimes went to visit. It was there, believe it or not, that we first heard of McDonald's Egg McMuffins. The McDonald's that was located about four blocks from the parsonage was one of the places that was a test market for the first fast-food breakfast. The egg sandwich and potato were the only choices offered at that time, along with orange juice and coffee. Pastor Rolfe and the boys would get up early on Saturday morning and walk down and have breakfast together, almost every time we visited. I am not sure why that day we were in Port Huron without them, but we were.

In was about two o'clock in the afternoon when the phone rang. Jeff was the only person in the house at the time. The female caller asked, "Do you know where your father is?" Jeff said that I was at Pastor Rolfe's. She then asked, "Do you know where your mother is?"

Jeff replied, "She is with my dad."

The voice then said, "No . . . I mean your real mother."

Jeff's reaction was to do what was comfortable for him or any of our children to do. He hung up the phone and ran the two blocks to my mother's house and told her what had happened. She called us immediately.

It was a long drive home. By the time we got there about two hours later, all three children and my mother were inside our house. We just waited for the phone to ring, wondering what changes were about to take place in the life of our family. The call that we believed was *inevitable*, one of Jeff's most famous words, was going to come soon. What did Patricia want? What had she done? What would our reaction be?

I am sure that I was thinking what decisions had been made. Did she petition the court? Had the judge done as he said that he would be required to do, give custody of our children to this woman they did not know, someone they had not seen or heard from in nearly thirteen years? What will the reaction of our children be?

As we sat there in our living room that Sunday evening, I could sense the tension building. I remember that I kept watching Darlene as she and the three children were talking. At that time, I was wondering, behind that calm, relaxed outer expression she was projecting, what was she really thinking? This young woman who came into our lives, with her eyes wide open, Darlene, who had not only taken on the responsibility of being a wife but also accepted becoming the mother of three young, insecure children, this beautiful woman who was so full of love and everything that I believed to be good, was now facing an unbelievable challenge. I was sure, that on the inside, she was more than a just a little nervous, this special angel who was not only willing to give herself for us, but also gave up her own priorities for my three children. I was reminded that we had a number of conversations about whether we would have other children. We had decided that we would just concentrate on being the best parents possible to Janet K, Randy J, and Jeffrey Glen. Soon after our marriage vows, Darlene had surgery, taking away any chance of ever giving birth to any other children.

The telephone rang about five o'clock. Patricia asked if she could come and see the children. I invited her to come and gave her directions. She arrived about an hour later. My remembrance of that evening was that all three children were curious. I am sure that they all wanted to know what she looked like. (I had no pictures of her.) We all sat in the living room. Conversation was awkward at best and did not last very long. Patricia did ask me if she could take the three children to Mason and buy them an ice cream cone. My reply obviously was no. She only stayed perhaps a total of an hour, an hour that created within me an indescribable amount of stress.

We sat there in the living room after she left, the five of us, and answered as best we could any and all the questions that anyone had. That night, after we had gone to bed, Darlene and I lie talking about what adjustments we might have to make in our lives and the lives of our children. I did my best to reassure Darlene that everything would be fine. I doubt that I believed that any more than she did. We had a pleasant surprise awaiting us from an unexpected source.

Over the years, I have picked up bits and pieces from them about what really happened in the minds of our children during those growing up years living with us in our home and just what they can remember. There certainly must have been times they can remember that their mom "actually" raised her voice. It is possible that there was a time or two that she even got angry. I'm sure that they can remember me sometimes as being unreasonable, maybe even more than a little strict and unbending in what I allowed them to do and where I allowed them to go. And yet I am confident that all three of our children have never doubted our love for them or our love for each other. As I developed my plan for writing what I remember of my life, I have certainly included mostly the good times because that is what I have chosen to remember. Actually, that is what I prefer to remember. Oh, I can remember the pain of getting hit by a truck and the fact that I lived many years with the fear that I would perhaps lose my children. I have lived during difficult times, physically and monetarily. But I have no recollection of any internal conflict within our family, and I don't remember any disobedience or rebellion from our children. The truth is that if I could remember, I wouldn't write about it anyway. I just want to remember the good times, of which there are many.

Janet had reached the age of sixteen. I really don't know whether she had ever been kissed (except by her dad, of course). What I am confident is that she is a wonderful daughter, as a teenager, and was not ashamed of her parents. Janet seemed always proud to have us attend her activities and to be a part of her life. She was always bringing her friends home, and we were very comfortable with her life. She was then and still is her daddy's *little girl.*

At the age of fifteen, Randy was perhaps one of the hardest working boys I have ever known. He seemed to thrive on working, not only at school (as a student custodian), but at home as well. Mowing the yard, keeping the garage clean, he was always ready and willing to work alongside me whenever he had the chance.

At thirteen, Jeff was well on his way to putting the emphasis that is necessary to be an outstanding basketball player. He spent countless hours shooting baskets outside at a basket we had put on the old barn turned garage. That spring we built a small concrete pad in the driveway that would keep him out of the mud. He was unbelievable, seemingly never tiring of shooting at the old hoop. I remember that one evening the two of us were playing twenty-one, the score had reached twenty to nothing, and I was not ahead. As Jeff drove, dribbling toward the basket for that final point, I wrapped my arms around him and said, "Jeff, you will never beat me twenty-one to nothing."

School was also important to Jeffrey. Getting good grades was very important to him. Even at that time police work was on his mind, a career he talked about from the time he was a preschool little boy until he left for college to get his degree in criminal justice. He had many friends and enjoyed reading everything he could find.

During those days, Darlene was teaching kindergarten at Dansville, where she came straight from college. It was the offer for a teaching position that Mr. Searl Briggs had sent her in the mail while she was still at Greenville College that God used it to send that *special angel* to us. By this time in her career, she had earned the respect of the community, especially of the parents of her students. The rest of her energy was used as a homemaker, wife, and mother. When not at work in the shop, my time was spent then working at home or involving myself in our children's activities.

As I reflect on those years, I believe that we were a family that was comfortable with who we were, where we were in our individual lives, as well as happy and contented as a family. It was a time in our lives that while we all were doing those things that were important, we took time for one another, time to be a family.

We had set aside Friday night as our family night. Each week, when it was my turn, I got $3 to spend and the choice of the family Friday night family activity. It would be my turn every fifth week, rotating with each member of the family. Each of us, I'm sure, have many memories of the good times that we had. We still enjoy just spending time together as a family. However, the number of family members has increased over the years, from five to fourteen. Life was good in the Cook household.

But what happened just three days after Patricia's surprise visit, after so many years, was totally unexpected, on the part of our visitor and on our eldest son as well.

It was mid-afternoon on Wednesday that Patricia drove up and parked in front of our house. The three children were all at home, and they went outside to talk with her. As Darlene stood looking out the window, at this woman she did not know and these three teenagers she had tried so hard to be the mother of, the woman they had never known nor heard from was walking around, laughing, and talking as if she was their long-lost friend (or mother). Darlene told me many months later that as she watched, she was frightened beyond belief. She wondered that if I had to make a choice between her and the children, who would be left behind? Would it be her?

As she continued to watch, with tears now streaming uncontrollably down her checks, she noticed that the mood had changed. There was no more laughing, Patricia was looking down toward the ground, and only Randy was talking. A few moments later, Patricia got into her car and drove away. A short time later, the three children came back inside the house. Our fifteen-year-old son, the boy, who sometimes, I believe, Darlene was somewhat afraid of, wrapped his arms around her and said,

"Mom, we told her that when we needed her, she was not around, and now we have all the mother that we need."

What more could three teenagers say to express how they felt about this woman who had given so much? What better way could they have expressed their feeling to Darlene as to who their mom was?

As Darlene told me about what had happened that afternoon when I arrived home from work that day, I could hardly believe it.

And yet as the years go by, and our children continue to mature, I have thought about that day many times. How could Randy, who I knew was speaking for Janet and Jeff as well, have said anything else? How could anyone ever have a better mother than Darlene, *God's special angel*? As time passed and looking back on our lives, the five of us, our children's spouses, and grandchildren as well, we are able to better understand how this special angel has affected each of our lives. I try never to think about what not only my life but also the lives of my children would be like if either Darlene or myself had not been open and obedient to God's leading. Certainly, I believe that Darlene was sent from above to love, to nurture, and to give a lifetime of mothering to each one of our children, grandchildren, and to be my life partner, as well as my wife.

God is good. It is his grace that is sufficient to keep us and protect us and to meet our every need in his time, not our time.

Chapter 12

Living Fear Free

This was a time for celebration, a time of victory, a time when I could put behind me the greatest fear that I had ever experience. For me, it was an unbelievable time of relief. For the first time since my children were just little babies, I could relax and be confident that they were not in danger of being taken from me. What Randy said about having "all the mother that they needed" certainly summed up in one sentence what Darlene had done for our children during the past ten years. I'm sure that as Randy, Janet, and Jeff were walking in our yard with Patricia, Randy did not realize the long-range impact that his statement would have on our family. Time has certainly proved him right. One of the greatest privileges I have enjoyed during my lifetime has been watching the continuing development between Darlene and our three children, who have grown up, married, and now have children of their own. Surely they realize now more than ever that Darlene has been, is, and will always be "all the mother that they need."

The years we spent in the village were very eventful. After working for General Motors for eleven years, I was heavily recruited to work for the school in Dansville. A five-year plan for remolding the school was going to be implemented, and the school board was going to act as their own general contractor. They needed someone to act as their eyes and ears working with all the various subcontractors, and they also wanted me to clean up a very broken-down and dirty school inside and out. It was during this time that our little children grew up. Janet was now driving our car, and Randy would not be far behind. Jeff joined his brother, and I was back working at the school. These were great experiences for me because I had time to be with the boys even when I was at work. I had decided to go back to the days when I worked as a student custodian, when students cleaned the entire school. I got the approval of the administration to hire as many boys as it would take to get the job done. I did hire Dick Carter to do maintenance work, such as boilers, leaking roofs, and electrical and plumbing repair.

My plan was to hire three students each spring as they finished the eighth grade. That year joining our staff were Jeff, Martin Perrine, and Chris Magsig. They were a great trio. As time passed, I had a staff of twelve student custodians, three in each high school grade. These boys not only provided Dansville with the cleanest school buildings around, but they also learned a great deal about doing the job right the first time. My goal for these students was to make their jobs important in their eyes and in the eyes of those around them. I wanted them to learn that whatever occupation in life they ended up with, it would be important. I knew that if I believed they were important, they would believe it too. I also wanted them to enjoy their work, and enjoy it they did. They liked being considered important by me, teachers, administrators, and staff members as well.

Not all their time was spent working. They played as well. Oftentimes they were sure they were getting away with pulling pranks on one another without me realizing it, or maybe sometimes they did. However, I oftentimes just looked the other way. After all, I too had been a student custodian. I knew all about chalkboard eraser fights and water pistol shootouts. I allowed them to be boys, but at the same time the amount of work that the school received for their wages was a bargain. The pride that each of these boys took in their work was beneficial to them then and later in their lives. Their work ethic gave them good training, I have no doubt. They also became my friends, and I look forward to hearing from them from time to time.

Working at the school was more than just a job to me. When I was a teenager, I wanted to be a high school history teacher. After graduating from high school, I got my priorities a little mixed up and never made it to college. Being in the school system gave me the opportunity to be a contributor to the education of boys and girl and young people. My goal when I first arrived on the job on July 5, 1974, was to restore the buildings and the grounds to the condition that I remembered them being in when I was a student there.

Gary Briggs, the brother of the school superintendent, had trained me when I had worked as a student custodian in the 1950s. I was determined to follow many of the same procedures he had so effectively used to make the buildings and the yards look so nice. Gary was still around at that time when I returned to the school to work and made several visits to my office to help me get started. My first hire was Randy. His job was to clean up the front of the buildings and kill the dandelions that had taken over the front yard. I needed him to edge the sidewalks, trim the scrubs, and make the front of the school look as nice as our front yard at home. He not only knew what needed to be done and how to do it, but he also did it.

Randy's efforts those first few weeks that summer did not go unnoticed. It is amazing what hard work and a lot of water can do to a lawn. As I turned my attention to the school's interior, I realized that it was going to take several years to get the buildings presentable. I decided to concentrate on the hallways, entranceways, and especially the windows that looked as if they had not been properly cleaned in years.

When school started that fall, it was immediately noticed by all that a change had taken place. Teachers were the most vocal, giving me compliments verbally and in the form of written notes. It was obvious that our school was looking better, it smelled better, and those who were there every day treated it better. I am absolutely convinced that it was the student custodians that made the difference. They competed with one another to see whose area would have the cleanest restrooms and the shiniest floors. These were sharp boys and good students who were very dependable, always on time, and rarely did any of them miss a day of work. The results were that we got the building properly cleaned every day, meeting and oftentimes exceeding the expectations of the faculty and the community.

I worked at the school for five years, and I enjoyed the teachers and the students very much. During those years, I had some really fun experiences as I worked alongside some great people. Perhaps a not-so-fun time was on Mother's Day in 1976. Some high school boys set the high school annex on fire at about four in the morning. I got the call at home that the school was on fire and that I need to get the gates open so the fire trucks could get in. As I rode my bike from our home up South Street, I could see the flames shooting into the night sky. I was sure that we were going to lose the entire school. As I was hurrying to get there, it looked like the three-story middle school was what was burning. It turned out to be only the annex to the high school. We only lost completely two classrooms, and the rest of the annex was a mess. Also, those guys had gone throughout the school, breaking interior windows and setting off powdered fire extinguishers. As the fire department was putting out the last of the fire, I convinced the school board that we needed to get our buildings ready so that we could have classes as usual on Monday morning. I believed then, as I do now, that we should not allow vandals to shut down our school. Although they voiced their doubt that it could be done, they asked me to try. That was all that I needed.

I have no doubt I was the only person in that meeting who believed it could be done. The more than $180,000 in damages could not stop us. Once again, I credit my student custodians and their parents, as well as Dick Carter. We got the job done. Certainly, today's union custodians would be asking if they would receive time and one half or double time, whether or not they thought it could be done, or if they wanted to work on Mother's Day. We had no time to stand around and talk about how big a job it would be, or how hard it would be, or even how much time it would take. My boys just dug in and did it. By eleven o'clock that night, we had moved out doors, scrubbed, and taken back into the classrooms every piece of furniture in the annex building; removed all broken glass in the elementary, middle, and high schools; cleaned and removed the fire extinguisher powder that was throughout the buildings. They also cleaned and polished all the hallway floors and cleaned every restroom. With our students' help, Dick Carter repainted two classrooms that had smoke damage. On Monday morning, Dansville Schools were open for business of educating boys and girls on time. Our students and teaching staff were there, and life went on as usual. I was proud of my staff of hardworking young men. Their work ethic skill, as well as their focus on the job at hand, made me proud. The guys won.

While I was working at the school, Janet and Randy graduated. These truly were good times for me and for our family. I served as president of the band promoters, heading a successful fundraising drive that allowed us to purchase new band uniforms. I also traveled to Florida with the band, along with Darlene and more than 350 other parents and friends. All three kids were in the band that year, even though Jeff was still in eighth grade. They performed before tens of thousands of people in competitions, such as marching, concerts, and precision drills. They won the Heart of St. Petersburg Award. It was a great experience for our family. There were many other band activities that we enjoyed as a family. Darlene and I always seemed welcome to be involved in whatever our children were involved in. We still feel that way.

Another benefit of working at the school during this time was having the opportunity to watch all our three children in their various school activities. I would see them every day, when they would stop by my office, in the hall, or at some student event. All three of them were making sure that her every need and want was met.

I liked just being there with the family, even if I didn't have a real important job in the eyes of most people. However, I believed that when teachers arrived in the morning to begin their day, if they found the doors unlocked, the lights on, the coffee made, if they walked on shiny floors, and their room smelled clean, they would be better teachers that day. If I could contribute to making that happen, then I believe my job was important. It mattered not whether anyone else understood that. I knew that I was making a difference.

I was especially pleased with the way we were able to improve the grounds around the school. My thinking was that many people who drive by or attend a baseball or football game might never enter our buildings. And yet they have an opinion on how their tax dollars are being spent and how our school is being cared for. I remember that I got Lewis Freer, a local farmer and friend, to bring his farm tractor and sprayer and kill the dandelions each spring. We focused on the lawns around the buildings the first summer, then the next year I decided to tackle the football field. What it needed was water. We rented a field tile trencher, and using three-inch plastic pipe, we ran a water line from the shop building all the way to the far side of the football field. I then purchased one of those tractor-watering sprinklers, like Randy bought me for my yard years later, and in late July, we started watering. We also had Mr. Freer spray for weeds and fertilize the whole football field every month. By the time football season was ready to start, the field was thick and green. We also built practice fields, one for the band and one for the football team. The football coaches and Mr. Francis, the band director, agreed to use them for practice and stay off the main field. The teams and the band as well wanted a playing field that they could be proud of. When we mowed the grass, we mowed every five yards, driving the mower in opposite directions, giving the field a stripped appearance. And when painted, it was beautiful. The stripes really made the five-yard lines show up and with the big white D on the 50 yard line. Dansville had a football field that everyone was proud of.

 I would probably still be working at the school if it were not for the politics of school boards. I loved the job, enjoyed the staff, and believed that I was a contributor to the education of the children and young people of the Dansville area. But I took another job in the fall of 1978. It was a good decision.

Chapter 13

Beginning A New Career

On the Monday following Thanksgiving Day in 1978, I became employed by a company in Jackson named Aalen Aides Inc. A position that would be the beginning of a new career, I was being hired as a salesperson with the challenge of selling cleaning supplies and equipment in the Ann Arbor area. This was for a company from whom I had purchased cleaning supplies while I was working at the school. It was certainly going to be a real change in my work responsibilities and be a real adjustment for our family and for myself as well. I remember that we all went out to dinner at one of our favorite restaurants, and it was there that I announced my decision to change jobs. My announcement was not well received by our children, which was a surprise to me. I thought that they would be excited, but then I realized how much they enjoyed having me working at the school. Darlene was beginning her fifteenth year of teaching, Janet was still at home working as a secretary at a doctor's office in East Lansing, Randy was living at home attending LCC, and Jeff was a senior in high school.

The new job was an exciting one for me. But then every job that I have ever had was rewarding and exciting to me. I was given a sales territory in the Ann Arbor area, selling in towns such as Dexter, Saline, and Milan, as well as Ann Arbor itself. My responsibility was to maintain and develop existing accounts and open new ones. We sold all kinds of cleaning products and equipment. I found that my experiences of using and buying products such as these were very helpful. I continued in this position until the following June, and then I was promoted.

The company decided to create a new position. They called it "Director of School Development." My business card read, "School Consultant." I was given the responsibility of calling on all the school accounts of the company. This included those that were located throughout the entire state. Because this was a new and untried position, they decided that I should receive a salary instead of depending on sales commission. It was a fun job, calling on people who had similar problems and challenges that I had while working in Dansville.

I had many great experiences during the following months and made many friends working as a school consultant. I was able to take selling to a different level, solving problems, sharing ideas, and providing products and equipment that would meet the customer needs. It was really fun. People ordered all kinds of stuff without thinking that I was really selling it to them. Of course, I needed to be sure that we did solve their problem. Perhaps one way that I made myself important was when I offered to refinish their wood gym floors without any charge, if I could use our products. It was, of course, the sale of the products to prepare the gym floor and the floor finish itself that made the job profitable. I had been trained to use an airless sprayer and could spray a normal-size gym in less than thirty minutes. This was as much as a two-day job for as many as four custodians. I have sprayed more than three thousand gym floors in my career so far. This has been a tremendous savings for my schools and very profitable for my company.

I continued in that position with the company for just about a year. I remember I had been working out of our Mount Pleasant office when I got a call from our president Philip Consolino. His father Tony wanted me to come as soon as possible to Jackson and meet him at his home. I called Darlene to tell her that I would be late getting home. It would be at least six o'clock before I reached Jackson. As I drove south from Lansing, I was wondering what I had done to cause them to want to see me. I certainly felt that I was doing my job. I believed that things were moving along very well. I remember thinking maybe this is the way Italians fire people, but for what?

When I arrived at Tony's home, Phil was there, along with the chairman of the board. As I sat down in Tony's living room, Phil brought me a TV tray and a large salad with the traditional oil and vinegar dressing, which I would soon learn was the only dressing that this Italian family ever served. As the three of us were eating, Phil and his father were just talking small talk, and I was eating my salad, trying not to look too nervous. After I had finished the salad, Phil brought me a huge plateful of linguine with clam sauce. I ate in silence, and as I sat there, I had no idea why I was there, nor did I have even a remote idea of what was about to happen.

Suddenly, Tony turned off the television, looked over at me, and said, "I need you to be my sales manager."

I looked at Phil and then at Tony, trying to buy a few seconds to get my composure. I then said, "Sir, I am honored that you would consider me for such a job, but what about Sam, Des, and all the others who have worked here much longer than I have?"

I learned something about Tony that evening, something that I would be reminded of many times in the years ahead. He banged his fist on the TV tray and said, "Sam and Des do not decide who is going to do what in my company." Tony then looked at me and said, "I'll decide, and I've decided that you are going to be sales manager, and they are going to like it."

I was really tongue-tied for one of the few times that I can ever remember before or since. I once again thanked Tony and then said, "I would like to go home and talk to Darlene about it and to pray about it."

Tony said, "I think that is a good idea, you do that."

Feeling a little better, I asked, "When do you need a decision from me?"

Tony said, "I am announcing your appointment tomorrow morning at the company's quarterly sales meeting at 7:00 a.m."

Well, as I drove home thinking about the meeting at Tony's home, I realized that I must have some skill that they had seen in me. I had at that time only been employed by Aalen Aides for one and a half years and was receiving what I assumed was to be a second promotion. As we talked about my new responsibility that night, Darlene asked, "What is your pay going to be?"

I had no idea. Neither of the Consolinos had even mentioned it, and I certainly would not have asked even if I had thought of it. At that time, I was earning about $20,000 a year, and I was being furnished a company compact station wagon like all the other salespeople. I had to pay $170 per month to the company for personal use of the vehicle. That was, by far, the most money I had ever made in my life.

The sales meeting that next morning was held at the Quality Inn in Jackson. It was a breakfast meeting, and the salespeople from our Mount Pleasant branch were at the meeting, along with the Jackson salespeople, and all five of the Consolino boys and their father. After the breakfast that we were served and that I was nervously trying to eat without looking nervous, aware that an announcement was soon to come, Tony stood and said in his blunt no-nonsense way, "I am naming, starting today, Jack Cook as our new sales manager."

The room grew silent, then Sam Rieder stood up, walked over to me, stuck out his hand, and said, "Congratulations! I am sure that you will do a great job, and you can count on me to do all that I can to help you succeed."

Everyone stood and applauded. I felt pretty good, especially about Sam who was one of those people most would call kind of special. He was never very friendly toward me, but other salespeople would tell me that was the way Sam was to everyone. The only person that Sam was interested in helping was Sam. Well, here he was, leading a standing ovation for me. It was years later that Sam confessed to me that Tony had called him the night before, telling him of my promotion, telling him to get up and congratulate me immediately.

This turned out to be a very exciting opportunity for me. The company sent Darlene and myself each year to ISSA conventions around the country, all expenses paid, places like Chicago, Montreal, Kansas City, Los Angeles, Dallas, Atlanta, New Orleans, New York, Las Vegas, and Houston. I was also given the opportunity to visit many manufacturing plants. This was helpful for me in understanding their strengths and weaknesses. Back home, at work, I had the responsibility of hiring and training new salespeople as well as being an encourager to our sales veterans. I certainly never lacked things to do. When I arrived at work the day that the announcement of my new position was made to the sales force, Tom Small brought me a set of car keys. He told me, "The blue Buick next to the building, that is your car now."

That uncovered a problem that would haunt me and cause me a great deal of grief for the rest of my career. The car that was mine to drive was a new huge four-door Buick. I don't remember the model. The problem was that the company had just bought it for David, one of the sons. He had fallen out of favor with Tony and had been transferred to the warehouse. David wasn't the problem. I don't think he was given my car to drive. However, his wife Jennifer was angry and did not sugarcoat her displeasure that I was given her husband's car. She never got over that, and other things that happened, she believed, as did all the sons' wives, that their husbands were always shortchanged by Tony Senior.

I believe that with the exception of one or two of them, they were getting a free ride. I seriously doubt that any of the sons would ever be able to have the positions that they enjoyed in the company, except for the fact that their father owned the company. Tony increased my salary to $25,000 and told me that they would try to give me a bonus at the end of the fiscal year. I was in a dream world as I starting up the corporate ladder. I found myself being promoted by the company as an important management team member to the industry throughout the country. I learned later that many of our largest manufacturers had expressed concern about the ability of the company to survive in a competitive marketplace after Tony who was in his mid-sixties.

As the years went by, we had good growth, buying a small company in Cadillac, complete with the former owner's home on Lake Cadillac. That stretched out my work area all the way to Traverse City. We were also showing good growth in our Jackson office.

Janet had taken a job at this time with the Felpausch Corporation, located in Hastings, with supermarkets all around Central Michigan. She arranged for me to do a demonstration in the Mason store for her manager. He sent me to Hastings and a meeting with Mark Feldpausch. Mark agreed to let me use Mason as a test store, and he hired our Jeff, who was at that time a student at LCC. Jeff went into the store each morning at 5:00 a.m. to clean the floor. With the results of this test and the help of Janet and Jeff, we landed the whole supermarket chain, the largest account that we as a company had ever had.

Success breeds success, which was true of our company. We continued to grow, becoming the largest company of our kind in the state of Michigan. Much of this, but not all, came from supermarket chains that were family-owned, small chain stores like Felpausch. Janet and Jeff's help was instrumental in expanding our ability to receive a great deal of new business. I continued to receive pay increases and perks that were allowing us to live in a style that we had never dreamed of. Randy and Jeff continued their education, transferring from LCC to Michigan State and Ferris State, respectively. Janet got married. I was certainly *feeling good*, and I was feeling good *even at work*.

Our children continued to develop their own lives, becoming more and more independent. They became less and less dependent on us for financial support. Randy graduated from Michigan State with honors, a feat that he accomplished because of a work ethic that had and would continue to serve him well. He and Belinda got married during the summer between his junior and senior year. Because he was unable to find a teaching opportunity in Michigan, even though he tried as hard as anyone that I have ever known, he finally decided to accept a position in Texas. This created a new challenge for me. I would be having one of my children out of my sight for the first time in their entire life. Jeff, after graduating from Ferris, became a police officer in Delhi, starting the career that had been his dream for as long as I can remember. He continued to live at home with us. Janet gave birth to our first grandchild. They named him Christopher Jacob. Darlene was continuing with her teaching career at Dansville. Aalen Aides continued to expand, buying a company in Traverse City and one in Dearborn as well, bringing to five the number of locations where we had employees and customers to care for.

My plate was far too full, with nineteen outside salespeople and inside customer service people in each location as well. I could feel myself choking on all the responsibility. We decided to relieve some of my traveling by hiring two field trainers. These men were to work with the outside salespeople, especially in the branches. I was continually given new titles, more responsibility, and more money. I found myself again and again sitting in corporate board meeting, the only non-family present. These meetings were held in the evening after the normal workday had ended.

I learned a great deal about family businesses during those board meetings. Titles meant nothing. Father-son relationship meant everything. Most of the time the sons were actually no more than just yes men, fearful of stating in meetings what I would hear them say privately. It became a game for me, watching the reaction that Tony would have as each department head reported their progress of their area of responsibility

I learned many lessons from Tony, lessons that have been very useful to me over the years in dealing with people and in motivating them to do what I want them to do. One of my favorite examples took place in one of those evening board meetings. Jon, who was the son sent to college to get a degree from Central Michigan University in accounting, enabling him to take care of the company books, was also a procrastinator, the likes of which I had never seen. At the end of each meeting, Tony would give an assignment to each of us, a project to do, and he would at the next meeting ask for a report on our progress. John would almost always have an excuse as to why he had not gotten his project done.

At this particular session, Tony was asking for our progress report. When he came to Johnny, as usual, John started to give the reason why he did not have anything to report. Tony became enraged. He was holding a Styrofoam cup in his hands, gripping it so hard that it had completely collapsed. He said to John knowing that all of us were listening, "Do you see this cup? Do you see this spoon, this fork, this knife? When I tell you to move the cup, don't tell me you didn't have time because you were moving the spoon, fork, or knife. MOVE. THE. CUP."

While I would never use the language that Tony used that night, I have used the story many times. Certainly, there is something to be said about understanding who is doing the asking and who is making the decision of what to do.

In the spring of 1989, Darlene and I purchased a home near Cadillac on Lake Mitchell. It was a year-around home that we did extensive remodeling to. When we were finished, we had a four-bedroom, two-bathroom home on the lake with 100 feet of lakefront property, a speedboat, and pontoon.

During this time, we had become the grandparents of six beautiful grandchildren, two girls and four boys. Each of our children had blessed us by giving us two grandchildren. I have many fond memories of our five or so years at that lakefront home. It was not only a place for me to relax, but also a place to spend quality time with our children and grandchildren. There was just something about being out on the lake with a fishing pole, not really caring if the fish were biting or not.

As I reflect on those days at the lake, I am sure that God used that time for us to draw continually closer as a family. We got to spend some precious time with our young grandchildren. Who could ever forget the time spent fishing, boating, or just playing together in the water and yard? We caught some nice fish. The ones that meant the most to me were all those we caught on the far side of the lake. When we left the dock, whichever grandchild was driving the pontoon boat would almost always decide that we needed to fish on the other side of the lake.

Because we had a live well on the boat, we could keep all the fish that we caught. When we returned to our dock, I would have the grandkids take the fish out of the live well and put them under our dock. We must have had most of the small fish in that lake under our dock at least once or twice.

Jennifer, who was pretty young, referred to our house on the lake as up north. To her it was up north, whether we were leaving from Mason or if we were out on the lake, and when she wanted to rest in her room, she would always ask us to take her up north. The three older boys—Chris, Phil, and Justin—liked to sleep outdoors in a tent at least part of the many nights they spend with us in that house. We have a lot of pictures and fond memories, but the cost of keeping this as a second home became prohibitive. Then things began to change at Aalen Aides.

I had been promoted to the position of executive vice president and general manager of the company, a job that was just too much for me to handle. I still had field trainers to work with salespeople, but the responsibility of hiring, training, and managing people in five locations was extremely difficult. However, I really loved my job. I especially was pleased at the growth we were having, the team spirit of the employees, and the satisfaction, which we were building, the best bottom-line profit in company history. I had convinced the team of department managers to forgo an increase in their salaries, and instead, we presented to the president a plan that would give bonuses for bottom-line profit generated.

There were six of these mostly young ambitious managers who rolled off their sleeves and went to work. Determined to show us what they could do, they worked as hard, sacrificed as much, and were as determined as a group of people I had ever known. The bonuses were to be determined by the amount of bottom-line dollars that the corporation earned during the fiscal year. Seven months into the year, it was obvious to all that these managers were going to receive several thousand dollars each for their effort. Then during the tenth month of the year, the president came to our staff meeting and announced that we had lost money the month before and that there would not be any bonus paid. I knew that there was something terribly wrong, and unfortunately, so did some of my managers. I waited several days to meet with the president.

When we did meet, I simply asked, "What was going on? Why would you make an announcement like that without any discussion with me beforehand?"

His answer was very troubling to me. I knew we were having an outstanding year, a year in which we were having record-setting profits. What I did not know was where the money was going. It was two months later, while I was studying the profit and loss statement, when I found an entry listing more than $50,000, which had been used to buy stock from John, who had left the company and moved to Florida. In all the years I had worked for the family, I had heard story after story of dishonest transactions about our company, people who worked there, companies that were our competitors, manufacturers who supplied us, and our customers as well, and I never believed it. They had always treated Darlene and our family and me so well. And yet there was no way to put a spin on what had been done and to ever be able to explain to myself, let alone those people who had earned those bonuses. I believed that I needed to take a stand, a stand that deep down inside I knew would cost me my position within the company and, without a doubt, my job.

I simply reworked the numbers, figured out the amount that the bonuses would have been, and asked Philip to pay the managers. His answer, "There will be no bonuses paid."

I stayed for five rocky months with the company, hoping against hope that they would change their mind.

During that time, I was made aware of other such decisions that had been made, some even affecting me. I knew that if I stayed, I was as guilty in the minds of our managers, as they were. In October, I resigned, leaving little doubt as to the reason, knowing that Aalen Aides, the largest janitorial supply house in Michigan, was doomed. It could not survive. I never thought that they would collapse just because I left, but I knew that when I left, other key people would leave as well. More than a dozen did leave within thirty days, including five of our department managers. One year later, Aalen Aides was sold by the chairman to Michigan Air Gas Company. It was a tragic ending to a good company. A company that was built by so many hardworking, good people was now destroyed. The reason for the demise, without a doubt, was greed. How destructive it can be when it controls people or organizations.

Chapter 14

Short Flight, Lasting Results

The lights were so bright, the truck so big, I put out my hand to try and stop it, and then I was flying. I felt my gloves fly off, and my glasses as well. I landed in a snowbank some 55 feet from where I had been struck by the truck as I stood on the shoulder of I-94 near Jackson.

Well, this was the second time that I was struck by a vehicle as a pedestrian, and here I am, still walking, with a little difficulty, some seventeen years later. But let me start at the beginning and share this chapter of my life that I remember it.

On Monday, February 11, I left Jackson, where my office was located. As the director of sales development for the Aalen Aides Corporation, a supplier of cleaning supplies and equipment, I was responsible for hiring, training, and motivating salespeople in our office in Jackson as well as offices in Mount Pleasant, Cadillac, Traverse City, and Westland. It was snowing as I headed up 127 north through Lansing. About 5 miles south of Alma, the snow, driven by a westerly wind, had lowered visibility to near zero. Suddenly, my car was struck from behind. As I spun out of control, I held my breath as a stainless steel milk tanker truck barely missed me as he passed me on the right. Well, my trunk needed to be wired shut, one taillight was broken, and the rear quarter panel needed to be pulled away from the rear tire. Then I was ready to be on my way to Mount Pleasant for my three-o'clock sales meeting. I did have a cut over my eye and a splitting headache.

As I left Mount Pleasant that evening, heading south to our home just east of Dansville, I was tired after a long day that began at my usual time of arriving at my office at 6:00 a.m. As I reached Lansing, I thought that I must have been seeing things, for coming straight at me in my lane on the divided expressway was a car with its headlights on bright. As my mind began to think about what I should do, my feet went into action and stepped on the brake, which sent me sliding sideways down the highway as the car traveling the wrong way, driven by I'm sure a drunken driver, barely missed the front of my car. At that point, I was wide awake and longing to get to the safety of our garage and into our warm bed for the night. I remember that when Darlene heard the garage door close and did not hear me come into the house, she opened the door and asked, "What was wrong?"

I replied, "Oh nothing." I was just glad to be home.

The next morning, February 12, at about five ten, Darlene kissed me goodbye, as was her custom every morning as I left our home for my office. Believe it or not, it was raining as I drove through Dansville heading south on my way toward Jackson to the office.

As I neared the entrance ramp to the I-94 expressway, the rain had turned to sleet. Driving down the ramp, a road that I had traveled six days a week for more than eight years, I was aware that the expressway was going to go immediately uphill. It was a glare of ice. As I reached the crest of the hill, I saw cars scattered everywhere, all over the highway and in the ditch as well. As I tried to stop, my car went into a spin, hitting the center guardrail head on. I bounced off and slammed into it on the driver's side, spun around and came to a stop with the car passenger's side against the guardrail. My first thought was, how would I fill out the insurance forms? How could I tell yesterday's accident from this morning's?

It was dark, it was sleeting, and there were disabled cars all over the place. All that I could think of was getting out of my car and getting into the ditch, where I felt I would be safe. There were two young men who had their trunk open down in the ditch, starting to light flares to slow down traffic. As I was walking toward them, I heard the sound of a truck, turned, saw the headlights, and I was soon in flight.

I heard all of them, yelling, "You killed him!" "Call an ambulance!" "Get some help!" "Where did that truck come from?" "What was he trying to do?" There were a lot of other words that I heard that I will not repeat.

As I landed, I fell into a snowbank feet first up to my knees. My first thoughts were that I didn't think that I was dead. I was sure that if I was dying, I should feel a stream of warm blood running out of my mouth and that I should be doing that little cough that I have seen cowboys do in those old western movies. I knew that I was alive, and I really thought that I was okay. I did have a great deal of pain in my legs and in my right arm. I remember thinking what a week this has been already, and it is only Tuesday morning.

As I lay there in the snow that cold February morning, lots of thoughts went through my mind. Most importantly, how was I going to let Darlene know without alarming her? As a number of people who had been involved in the multi-car accident on the expressway began to gather around me, covering me with their coats, a man asked me whom he could contact. I asked him to take a business card from my suit coat pocket and go to Aalen Aides and ask for Phil. I was sure that he would be in the office by this time.

Darlene, who seldom called me at the office, either because of her women's intuition or because God spoke to her in her devotions that morning, called our office at six-oh-five and asked Phil if I had arrived yet. As he was telling her that he had not seen me yet, the man from the accident scene arrived, asking if anyone knew Jack Cook. Phil relayed the message that I was okay, that I had been in an accident, and that then I had been struck by a truck. Philip, whom we knew as a very compassionate person, told Darlene that she was to stay at home, the roads were icy, and that he would come and get her and take her to the hospital. He also called his father Tony, the chairman of the board and owner of our company, and asked him to be at the hospital when the ambulance arrived.

I could see the police cars and the emergency vehicles up on the Elm Street overpass. The problem was because of the traffic backups, they could not get down the ramp on to the expressway where I was. It was about seven thirty that morning when I finally arrived at Foote Hospital, cold beyond belief from lying packed in snow and covered with sleet for nearly two hours. I would never forget the gentleness of the people in the emergency room. They removed my outer clothing and covered me with blankets that had been in a warming oven. I was sure that I had died and gone to heaven. Unfortunately, that was about the only thing that went right during my stay at the hospital.

The cold certainly numbed the pain in my legs and my right arm. However, as I began to get warm, I was sure that there were problems with my legs, especially the left knee. It seemed like forever that I just laid there talking to Tony, who, by the way, had arrived at the hospital before me and was there waiting. Darlene and Phil arrived, and we waited, and we waited. Finally, they decided to take X-rays of my right arm and my legs. The left knee was definitely severely damaged.

The right leg and my right arm were just bruised, and I also had several contusions. They asked me if I had an orthopedic surgeon. Obviously, I did not. So into our lives came a Jackson resident orthopedic surgeon, Doctor Schneider. After several moments of examination and after looking at my X-rays, Doctor Schneider said that I needed to have surgery on my knee. However, because I was in a state of shock, he wanted to wait a day or two until I was more stable. On Thursday evening, he did surgery on my left knee, inserting a pin to hold the bones in place. While the pain continued, there was good reason to believe that I was on the mend.

On Sunday afternoon, Darlene and my brother Larry and his wife Sharon were visiting me. I was still on morphine for pain and not feeling well at all. In mid-afternoon, they decided to go down to the cafeteria for coffee. While they were gone, I felt extreme pain in my chest and was hot all over. I rang the bell, and people came from everywhere. They began injecting me in both arms at the same time and took me immediately to X-ray. They told me that I had developed embolisms (blood clots) in both lungs. It was about ten that evening when Doctor Schneider arrived in my room. Darlene was still there waiting to ask him what kind of treatment I would be receiving. The doctor stated that I was being constantly monitored and that they had me on a potent blood thinner. He told me that I must remain in bed flat on my back for about three weeks, that if I tried to get up to use the bathroom, I would be dead before I got there. That really did get my attention. The doctor also said that it was extremely important that I take no medication of any kind, except for what was being given to me through the tubes in my arms, not even aspirin. Well, that really changed things. Now my life was in danger, and I was constantly being monitored with all kinds of equipment attached to me. I really don't think that I slept well that night, but just before dawn, the lights came on, and a lady came into my room and announced that she was taking me down to physical therapy. When I told her that I was not to get out of bed, she assured me that I was to go with her. It took all my selling skills to convince her to go to the nurse station and check out my status. She did not return. However, a few hours later, when our daughter Janet was sitting beside my bed, a nurse came into my room with small cup with several pills and capsules in it. She said, "It's time for your medication."

Janet, in her firm way, informed the nurse that I was not to receive any medication, except for what was being given through the injections in my arms. The nurse was quite persistent, and Janet insisted that they call the doctor. The nurse reluctantly agreed as Janet followed her to the nurse's station to make the call. For the first time, I began to fear for my safety. Well, the medical records were updated, and Doctor Schneider assured me that everything would be fine. Our son Jeff wanted to, as he put it, get me out of this place. I was released three weeks later. With my leg in a cast and getting around in a wheelchair, I returned to work on my way home to conduct a company-wide sales meeting. The cast was removed a few weeks later, and I was driven to Jackson each day to have physical therapy. After several weeks of little or no response, Doctor Schneider suggested that I have outpatient surgery. The way the doctor explained it, because of the blood clots, the knee was not responding to the therapy. The lack of movement reduced the bend to less than 50 degrees. About 110 degrees of bend were necessary to walk without a limp. During these months, between February and May, I was taking, as directed by Doctor Schneider, Coumadin, a blood thinner, at exactly six o'clock each evening to keep my blood thin enough so that I would not pass any more clots from my leg to my heart, brain, or lungs.

Well, in mid-May, we agreed to have the surgery. Once again, we would visit Foote Hospital, this time by our choice (that was where Doctor Schneider did all his surgeries). On the day preceding the surgery, I was instructed to go to Foote and make out papers for pre-admittance. After giving my medical history, I listed all the medications I was currently taking. I arrived at the hospital at 7:00 a.m. as instructed, I was given a room, and after getting on the traditional hospital gown, they gave me something to sedate me. About eight thirty, they took me down to surgery. The procedure, as explained to us by the doctor, was to put me to sleep, and then the doctor would bend my knee and break loose all the adhesions restricting my knee and not allowing it to bend properly. Doctor Schneider told Darlene that I would feel a considerable amount of discomfort for several days. However, he was sure that this manipulation of the knee would give me unrestricted use of my left leg. We left the hospital at about five in the afternoon, stopping by the drug store in Paka Plaza to pick up prescriptions for pain and also my Coumadin.

Considerable discomfort was really an understatement. The pain in my leg was almost unbearable. The pain medication helped a lot, and I slept that night in my recliner to keep my foot elevated and relieved some of the throbbing. Our eldest grandson Christopher was my helper the next day so that Darlene could go to school. He seemed to always be close by whenever I need some help, and a big help he was, waiting on me hand and foot. I only got out of my chair to use the restroom. By late afternoon, I began to feel really strange. I can't explain it, except to say that I believe that our body tells us when something is wrong, and I was starting to believe my body, even though I certainly didn't know what the problem was. That evening Sharon, Larry's wife who lived next door, came over with her medical book. She and Darlene decided that perhaps I was suffering the side effects from the pain medication. Darlene called Doctor Schneider, and he reminded her that he had told her that I was going to have a lot of discomfort for a few days. He was sure that I would be fine.

The next day Chris was still caring for my every need. As the day wore on, I realized that every time that I stood up to go to the bathroom, I would feel dizzy and that there was a ringing in my ears.

That afternoon, when Darlene came home from school, once again, I told her that something was not right. I not only had a lot of pain, but I also just didn't feel very good. I told her about being dizzy and about the ringing in my ears when I stood up. She once again called our doctor. Once again, Doctor Schneider told her, only this time very firmly, that I would be just fine in two or three days. When Darlene asked about the ringing in my ears, his reply was "I don't know about the ringing in his ears, but trust me, he will be fine."

The following day my mom wanted to come any take care of me. Like all caring mothers, she was sure that she could lift my spirits and nurse me back to good health. Well, the problem was that by the time she arrived, I really felt sick. If I raised my head off my pillow, the ringing started, and I, at first, would just be dizzy, but by early afternoon, I would faint lying flat on my back in bed. I don't remember much after that, except that I kept thinking that Darlene would be home soon and then everything would be just fine. When Darlene arrived home, she took one look at me and immediately called the doctor's office; the doctor was out. However, the nurse told her she would find him and have him call.

About ten minutes later, the phone rang, and when Darlene answered it, Doctor Schneider asked, "What is it this time, Mrs. Cook?"

Gentle, soft-spoken Darlene told me later that she really got angry. My mother, some years later, told me she didn't know she could speak in that strong of a voice. Darlene said she told the doctor that there was something seriously wrong with me. I was ash-colored, unable to hold up my head without fainting, and that she wanted something done. Doctor Schneider suggested that she bring me into the office. Darlene replied, "He can't even get out of bed."

That was obviously when the light came on in the doctor's head. He asked, "Has Jack taken his Coumadin today?"

Darlene reminded him that I didn't take it until six o'clock. Doctor Schneider told her to call for an ambulance and that he would meet us at the hospital. So once again, I was headed for Foote Hospital. By this time, I was nearly unconscious, and I really don't remember the ride.

When we arrived in Jackson, the doctor was waiting. He knew what the problem was and had blood ready for a transfusion. I was bleeding internally from the Coumadin that I should have been taken off before the surgery. In all that night and early morning the next day, I received five blood transfusions. After twenty-one days in that hospital, my weight had dropped to less than a 120 pounds. I left the hospital once again with my leg still unable to bend enough to allow me to walk without crutches.

To say that I was discouraged would be an understatement. For a guy who loved to run the bases in a softball game, to actively be involved with my children and grandchildren, it was really discouraging to walk around the yard on crutches. Work, even for a company that was caring and understanding, was becoming very difficult. Worst of all, I was just about ready to accept the fact that I would never walk again without some form of support. I remember a Sunday afternoon when walking around our yard, I decided that it was all in my head. I decided to lay down my crutches and run across the yard, where no one could see me. I really believed that I could do it, so I tried. After two steps, I was lying face down in the grass, sobbing like a baby. I have never been any closer to giving up on myself as I did that day. But good things happen to those who believe. I just needed someone to lift me and restore my ability to believe that I could once again walk.

Chapter 15

Grandchildren And Great Grandchildren

At this time in our lives, Darlene and I have nine grandchildren and eleven great-grandchildren, and what a wonderful blessing they are.

Janet and Brian's two sons are the eldest. Both boys have master's degrees. Christopher met his wife Christen at Olivet College. Upon graduation, they married at our Nazarene church in Lansing. They spent the next few years in Texas, where Chris taught and Christen continued her education, earning her master's and doctorate from the University of Texas. Chris also received his master's degree in administration while he was teaching there. Christopher interviewed and was hired as elementary principal at Portland, Michigan, and Kristen began practicing in Holt as a doctor of therapy. They are parents of two of our great-grandchildren, seven-year-old Addison and five-month-old Ella.

Philip is special in that it took a while for him to decide what he wanted to do with his life. Once he made up his mind, he became an overnight success, earning his bachelor's degree from Grand Valley and his master's degree from Northern Illinois University. His wife

Kasey followed, earning both of the degrees her husband did. They are geologists currently in Bakersfield, California.

Phil and Kasey are proud parents of our other three great-grandchildren: Lily who is two and twins Max and June, ten-month-old babies. It is a busy household, I'm sure.

They started their career in the oil business in Houston, Texas. Phil's job was two locate exactly where the oil wells were to be drilled. He was either really good or lucky or maybe a little of both. The results were unbelievably successful, in fact, so successful the company paid him a huge bonus to take his talent across the country to their oil fields in Bakersfield, California.

We are proud of their success, but we really miss seeing them. They did come to Michigan for a few days last Summer, but they are a long way from home. Kasey does post pictures of the three children on Facebook, and Janet forwards pictures and messages to us regularly.

After several years of trying without success, Randy and his wife decided to adopt a child. While it seemed to take a long time, and there were so many hoops to jump through, it finally happened. Justin joined our family, a beautiful three-day-old little boy. Sister Mallory joined Justin three years later. From day on, we knew that Justin would be exciting to be around. He was and still is a live wire, sometimes an electric live wire even. As he grew and grew and grew some more, he soon would tower over all the other Cook boys and men. As is with so many big a guys, Justin is a gentleman with a smile that warms your heart. In middle school, he played football as a defensive lineman. The problem was that after he broke up the other team's play and tackled the ball carrier, he would apologize and be sorry for hurting him. He and his dad decided that maybe football was not a sport the he would enjoy, so they switched to basketball. Justin did well and played all the way through school at Mason.

After graduation, Justin decided to go to Western Michigan University. He did very well there and soon after graduation, settled into a good job in Jackson as the western third of the country's sales representative, hiring various firms to represent his company's product line. We are proud of Justin and always enjoy his visits, his smile, and his wit.

Jennifer is our eldest granddaughter. Her parents Jeff and Glenda have lived next door to us for more than twenty years. Jen is blond and has always liked blond jokes. In fact, I think she enjoys a good laugh anytime. As a young girl, she and her mother played with dolls a lot, especially the American Girl dolls. Her brother, Thomas Jack, joined her when she was three years old and has been a great sister to Tom, always making sure that he is getting the best of the best.

Long before high school, we recognized that Jennifer had not only a sharp mind but also a strong desire to excel. Her parents did well in school, and she would surpass even their achievements, graduating as the valedictorian of her Mason High School class.

Growing up in a Christian home and attending the Nazarene church, we were sure that she would go to Olivet University. However, even though many of her close friends went there, she chose to go to Grand valley. What a great choice. It was there she met Ken Spicer, a really great guy. They were married in the college chapel and chose to live in Grand Rapids, where Ken, after graduation, was hired by Amway as a computer tech. Jennifer enrolled in Michigan State University Medical School. She is scheduled to graduate after seven long years and will receive her MD degree this March.

Mallory came into our lives as literally a crybaby. She had a severe case of colic and cried a great deal during most of her waking hours. Well, she got it all out of her system while she was just a baby and has turned into a happy and exciting young lady. She was a daddy's girl, if I ever saw one. They seemed to be inseparable. Even when he was vacuuming the carpet, she would be riding the vacuum. Mallory (or Bug as her dad called her) started gymnastics at a very young age and spent far too many hours at practice and traveling around the state to compete. She continued to successfully advance her skill until, by ninth grade, she just tired of the sport. Her high school friend convinced her that she should be on the swim team as their diver. After all, as soon as you leave the dive board, it becomes gymnastics. She broke the school record at her first meet. Mallory was on her way to a full-ride scholarship at Michigan State, when while diving off the high board, she hit her head on the way down, ending her dreams as well as her diving career.

Setbacks didn't slow down our Mallory. She just changed directions, putting her boundless energy into a new venture. She enrolled at Douglas J Hair School and has become an outstanding cosmetologist. I believe that Mallory will be successful at whatever she chooses, and her fiancé Austin is the kind of guy who will always be by her side to give her the support she needs.

Thomas Jack joined his big sister Jennifer when Jen was three years old. As a child, it was Tom's smile that was his biggest asset. As he grew older, we realized that he was exceptionally intelligent. After finishing near the top of his class at Mason High School, he went to LCC, transferred and graduated with honors at Michigan State University.

I had the privilege of having Thomas work with me during one of his summer vacations while in college. I was rebuilding a house that I bought to fix up and sell. I have never seen anyone who learned so fast and worked so hard as Tom did that summer. He never missed a day of work, and he was always ten minutes early, something that I have spent years training employees to do. I really learned a lot about him and enjoyed listening to him talk about his interest in US history. Lucky for us, Thomas still lives next door and keeps our lawn mowed in the summer and our driveway cleared in the winter.

After college, Thomas got a job working at the airport in Lansing and then acquired a position at Lorain Oils in Lansing, a company that ships flavored oils all over the world. Thomas is getting a lot of experience in all aspects of the company experience that I'm sure will be beneficial in the future.

We have eleven great-grandchildren: five are Janet's, and six are Randy's. The eldest Addison was born, while Christopher and Kristin (Doctor Kenroy) were living in San Antonio, Texas. Each year, in January, we would visit them and enjoy their company, a trip or two to the Alamo, the Home show, and various other attractions, of which there were many. Each year it seemed that we would stay a little longer. One year, as we were preparing to leave, I said to Chris, "Find us a house near you, and we will buy it."

He took me seriously, and every couple of weeks he would send some pictures of a house that was for sale.

Their second little girl Ella was born after they moved back to Michigan.

Philip and Kasey have a two-year-old daughter, Lily, and last February, they became proud parents of twins Max and June. Living in California makes seeing them difficult. However, they come home as often as they are able.

We were certainly privileged to have had all six of our grandchildren living less than ten minutes away until they got out of high school. Great-grandchildren, we don't know them, and certainly, they don't know us. We think that is a shame. Oh well, what can two old people do about it?

Chapter 16

Retirement, Well, Kind Of

After the children all married and I was feeling a lot of pain from the accident in Jackson, we decided that I should retire. That didn't last very long. After two back surgeries and a resodamie, I felt as good as new.

I connected with a realtor whose wife was a principal at Randy's school. He paid me to fix up houses that he was going to list for sale. My job, make them attractive inside and out and ready to sell. I also decided to try my skill at flipping some bank-owned houses. I bought two houses in the next two years, and with the help of our grandsons Thomas and Justin, we turned them into very marketable properties. I sold them with land contracts at a good interest rate for me and a five-year balloon (balance of selling price was due in full within five-year period). Both families were able to meet the terms of the contract.

The profits from the sale of the two houses we sold were used to buy a second home in San Antonio, Texas. We enjoyed our time there, except for a few scary moments.

While getting my hair cut at my winter barbershop, my heart stopped. There just happened to be a nurse getting his haircut in the chair next to mine. The next thing I remember I knew that I was in a moving vehicle, I felt someone sticking a needle in both of my arms, and I heard someone say, "We have his blood pressure up to forty over twenty..."

Then I was at the Methodist Heart Hospital. Three days later, it stopped again, this time I aspirated (the contents of my stomach went into my lungs). This caused very serious pneumonia. Darlene called our children, and they flew to Texas, joining her at my bedside in the intensive care unit. Near death for the next four days, I survived, thanks to the doctor, who, for the next ten days, gave me what he called antibiotic cocktails. After thirty-one days, I was released to go home after they installed a pacemaker in my upper chest.

At the insistence of our children, I made an appointment at the Cleveland Heart Clinic. We made five trips there over the next few weeks. After numerous tests, it was decided to replace my aorta valve. They said it was from a pig. When I saw the bill, I tried to convince them that I at least should get the whole pig, considering what they charged. However, I never did get the pig.

Returning home to Michigan, I was watched very closely by Darlene and the children. I certainly enjoyed all the attention. Jeff got acquainted with a Calhoun county reserve police officer, who, he found out, was a retired cardiologist from the Cleveland Clinic. As Jeff shared with him how I was often feeling extremely tired, had trouble some days of just getting out of bed, Charles said that I needed to see the best cardiologist in the world. He lives in Japan. Jeff told him that he didn't think that I would be willing to go to Japan. Charles called the Mayo Clinic, where Dr. Nishimura came once a month to see cases like mine. Two weeks later, Darlene and I were in Rochester, Minnesota, meeting Dr. Nishimura.

We stayed at the clinic for eleven days, and after numerous tests, it was decided to insert a three-phase pacemaker, replacing the unit I received two years previously. Dr. Nishimura said that I should begin to feel better within two or three weeks. Well, I felt better instantly. We left Mayo clinic on Tuesday, but before we left for home, we met with Dr. Nishimura one more time. He asked me to write him a letter in thirty days, telling him how I felt. Later that week, on Friday evening, about eight o'clock, I received a phone call from Dr. Nishimura, checking on how I was feeling. He visited with me as if we were ole friends to say that I was impressed would be an understatement.

Chris and Kristin decided to move to Michigan. Doctor Kenroy took a position with a physical therapy office in Holt. Christopher accepted a principal's position in Portland, Michigan. We were so happy to have them, along with our great-granddaughter Addison, nearby. However, it did create a problem with our children who were concerned about us spending the winters in Texas with no family there.

After much discussion, it was decided that it would be best to sell our San Antonio home. We enjoyed Texas very much and made a number of friends, mostly at the small Nazarene church that we attended during our five years there. We really enjoined our home and yard. I liked picking fresh fruit from the trees in our backyard. We had grapefruit, orange, lemon, and tangerine trees that produced a large crop of fruit every winter. We also enjoyed the flowers in our yard, especially the many different kinds of roses that bloomed profusely. I remember that one day in April, just before we were planning to leave for Michigan, a car stopped in front of the house. I was working in the front flowerbed, when the driver walked over toward me and said that she had a sign to put in our yard. Believing her to be a political campaign worker, I asked, "Which party?"

She replied, "It isn't a political sign," as she placed the sign in the yard, which read, "YARD OF THE MONTH."

I thanked her, got my camera, and took a picture. It felt good to know that other people recognize all our hard work.

San Antonio's population is about 70 percent Hispanic. In fact, Texas is the only state where Caucasians are the minority. We made many friends that were of the Hispanic culture. We found them to not only be hard workers, but also have a close relationship within their families and friends. We still keep in touch with several families through Facebook.

We sold the house for our asking price in just two weeks after it was listed. The buyer was a young single man, his first home. Even though it was a sad time leaving Texas, Darlene and I have many fond memories of our time there. The last two years, we have wintered in Phoenix, Arizona, to be near our good friends, the Whitakers. Doug and Erma attend church with us here in Michigan, and live just a few miles west of us. We really enjoy their company and have taken several day trips with them, as well as spending several days together in Washington DC.

I am now eighty-seven years old. Darlene, of course, is much younger. We are enjoying life together and will continue to do so, regardless of where we are living. What a privilege it is that we not only love each other but also genuinely like each other. After nearly sixty years of marriage, Darlene remains that special angel whom God sent way back in 1964 to watch over me and our children. Her responsibilities have grown significantly; she not only cares for an aging husband and our three children and their spouses but also for nine grandchildren and eleven great-grandchildren.

Our three children and their families are doing well. Not only do we have grandchildren to love and spoil, but we have also lived long enough to have great-grandchildren.

As I reflect on my life...

I am a middle child in a family of fifteen children who love each other dearly. I was raised by hard-working parents who set an exemplary standard for us on how to live life, focusing on the good, the possible, and the happiness that comes from loving and being loved. I have friends who stand by me not only during the good times but also when life's road is filled with bumps and potholes. I am part of a church that believes as I do, that our God created all that is, was, and will ever be. This God sent his Son to die for my sins and rose again, ready and willing to come again when God the Father determines that the time is right... someday soon. Lastly, we have children, grandchildren, and great-grandchildren who live close by, and we enjoy hearing about their successes, challenges, as well as their dreams for the future.

Certainly, we have been blessed, even though we have had a few bumps in this road called life. There have been some anxious moments, more than a little pain, and some sadness as well, yet I can say without hesitation, 'Oh yes, GOD IS GOOD.'

And I have so many reasons why I AM FEELING GOOD... ALL THE TIME.